Wishniaore - 2006
FROM MAMUTZKA

QUESTIONS AND ANSWERS
WILD WILD
WORLD

This is a Parragon Publishing book
This edition published in 2006

Parragon Publishing
Queen Street House
4 Queen Street
Bath BA1 1HE, UK

Copyright © Parragon Books Ltd 2001

British Library Cataloguing-in-Publication Data

A catalogue record for this book is available from the British Library.

ISBN 1-40541-541-X

Printed in China

Originally produced by David West Children's Books
This edition by Design Principals

Illustrators James Field Sarah Lees Terry Riley Ross Watton (SGA) Rob Shone
Cartoonist Peter Wilks (SGA)
Editor James Pickering *Consultant* Steve Parker

QUESTIONS AND ANSWERS

WILD WILD WORLD

Written by

Anita Ganeri

Clare Oliver

Denny Robson

Contents

CHAPTER THREE
SNAKES AND OTHER REPTILES

CHAPTER FOUR
SHARKS AND OTHER DANGEROUS FISH

173 Who hides a feast in the trees?

174 How can you tell small cats from big?

174 Which cat barks?

175 Which cat has the most kittens?

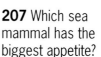

176 Do hyenas laugh?

177 Do hyena cubs get on together?

177 Do hyenas hunt?

178 How do dogs hunt?

178 Do dogs use babysitters?

179 What do pups eat?

180 What changes its coat in the winter?

180 Who's at home in the city?

181 Who won the race, the fox or the hare?

182 Which is the biggest dog?

183 Do wolves howl at the Moon?

183 Which wolf walks on stilts?

184 Which is the biggest bear?

185 Which cubs drink the creamiest milk?

185 Can bears walk on water?

186 Which bear fishes for its supper?

186 When do bears climb trees?

187 Do all bears eat meat?

188 Where can you see bears close-up?

189 How do dogs help people?

189 Where can you see big cats close-up?

CHAPTER SEVEN
WHALES AND OTHER SEA MAMMALS

192 What are sea mammals?

193 Which special features help whales live in the sea?

193 Which is the biggest sea mammal?

194 Do all whales have teeth?

195 What has tiny shellfish on its back?

195 What's the difference between whales and dolphins?

196 What do walruses use their tusks for?

196 Which seal blows up balloons?

197 Which seals live at the ends of the Earth?

198 Where do manatees and dugongs live?

199 How can you tell manatees and dugongs apart?

199 Which sea mammals are vegetarians?

200 Which sea mammal can swim the fastest?

201 Which is the speediest seal?

201 What is one of the deepest divers?

202 Which whales turn somersaults in the air?

202 Which sea mammals walk with their teeth?

203 Which sea mammals make the longest journey?

204 Which are the most intelligent sea mammals?

204 Which seal has a huge nose?

205 Why do whales sing to each other?

206 Which whale has the longest 'teeth'?

206 How do leopard seals catch their prey?

207 Which sea mammal has the biggest appetite?

208 What finds food with its whiskers?

208 Which sea mammals use fishing nets?

209 What uses a ceiling of water to catch fish?

210 How can you tell humpback whales apart?

211 Why are killer whales black and white?

211 Which whales change color as they grow up?

212 Which are the biggest sea mammal babies?

212 Which sea mammals live in a pod?

213 Which sea mammals live the longest?

CHAPTER EIGHT
GORILLAS AND OTHER PRIMATES

CHAPTER ONE

DINOSAURS

AND OTHER PREHISTORIC REPTILES

What were the dinosaurs?

Dinosaurs were reptiles of many amazing shapes and sizes that lived long ago. They had just the same needs as the animals you know today – to hunt, feed, breed and escape their enemies.

Herrerasaurus

Triassic   Jurassic

Is it true?

Dinosaurs only lived on land.

YES. They were adapted for life on land because they walked with straight legs tucked underneath their bodies, as we do. This gave them an advantage over other animals and helped them dominate the land.

Where did they live?

Everywhere on Earth, but the planet was completely different in dinosaur times. The seas, plants, animals and continents, Laurasia and Gondwana, were all different. And there were no people!

Laurasia

Gondwana

Cretaceous

When did they live?

Dinosaurs ruled the world for millions of years. They appeared about 225 million years ago and died out 65 million years ago. There were three periods in dinosaur history: Triassic, when the first dinosaurs appeared; Jurassic and Cretaceous, when dinosaurs dominated the land.

Amazing! One of the earliest dinosaurs ever found was Eoraptor, 'dawn stealer', and it lived 225 million years ago. It was only three feet long and probably a fierce hunter of small reptiles.

Eoraptor

Were there any other animals?

Insects, small mammals and many modern forms of life lived in the shadow of the dinosaurs, as well as other reptiles. Pterosaurs soared through the air, while ichthyosaurs and plesiosaurs swam in the seas.

Pterosaurs

Plesiosaur

Ichthyosaur

Where did dinosaurs come from?

There was life on Earth for over 3,000 million years before the dinosaurs. Mammal-like reptiles were living on the land just before the dinosaurs appeared. Some scientists think Lagosuchus (which means rabbit crocodile) was the ancestor of all dinosaurs.

Lagosuchus

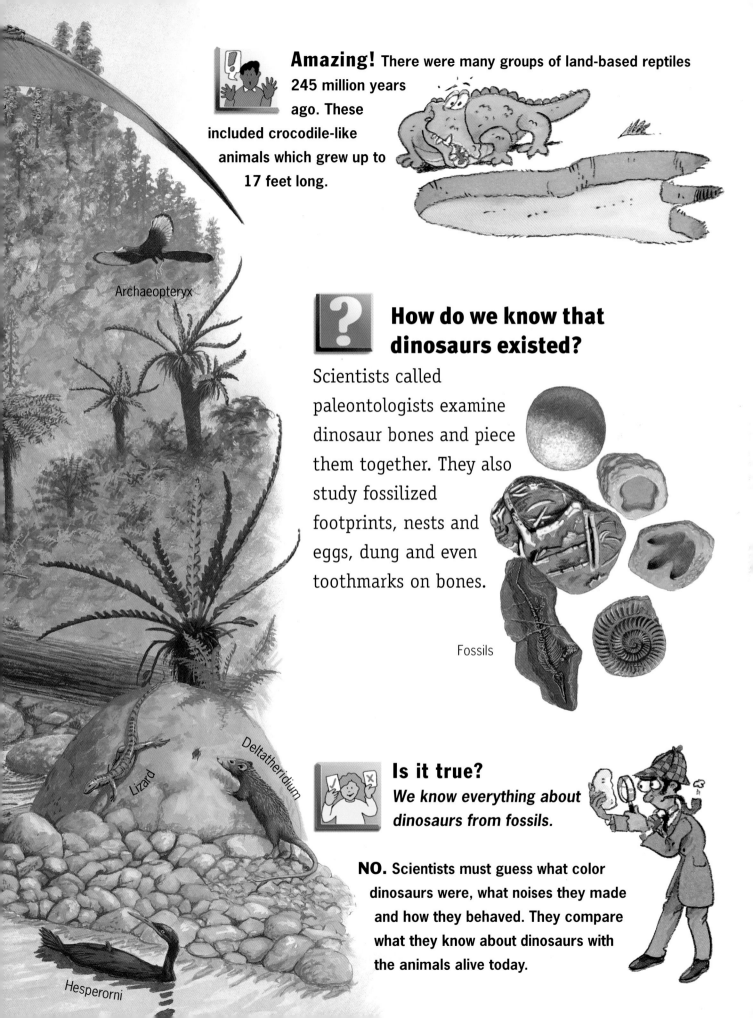

Amazing! There were many groups of land-based reptiles 245 million years ago. These included crocodile-like animals which grew up to 17 feet long.

Archaeopteryx

Lizard

Deltatheridium

Hesperorni

How do we know that dinosaurs existed?

Scientists called paleontologists examine dinosaur bones and piece them together. They also study fossilized footprints, nests and eggs, dung and even toothmarks on bones.

Fossils

Is it true?
We know everything about dinosaurs from fossils.

NO. Scientists must guess what color dinosaurs were, what noises they made and how they behaved. They compare what they know about dinosaurs with the animals alive today.

Which were the biggest dinosaurs?

In the Jurassic age, giant plant eaters called sauropods became the largest animals to walk on Earth. One of them, Ultrasauros, may have been up to 100 feet long and about 60 feet high, which is as tall as a six-story building!

Is it true?
All sauropods were huge and wide.

NO. Sauropods were huge, but some were 'slim'. This helped when they walked through woods looking for food.

Compsognathus

Which were the smallest dinosaurs?

Compsognathus was the size of a turkey and weighed about six pounds. It hunted insects and lizards. Heterodontosaurus and Lesothosaurus, both plant-eating dinosaurs, were just as small.

16

? Which were the heaviest dinosaurs?

Ultrasauros may have weighed as much as 50 tons, but scientists have recently found evidence of an even bigger dinosaur in Argentina. The gigantic Argentinosaurus may have weighed as much as 100 tons. Most sauropods were smaller, weighing between 30 and 80 tons.

Ultrasauros

Amazing! The neck of Mamenchisaurus was 50 feet long, strengthened by a system of spines. It could not have been lifted very high. Mamenchisaurus probably fed on low-growing vegetation.

? How do we know which dinosaurs ate meat, and which ate plants?

We can tell by looking at fossils of their teeth and claws. Meat eaters and plant eaters developed different special features, such as hands that could grasp and grinding or shearing teeth.

Plant eater fossil

Meat eater fossil

Yunnanosaurus

? What were plant eaters' teeth like?

Yunnanosaurus had chisel-like teeth to cut up tough vegetation. Some sauropods had spoon-shaped teeth for cutting tough plants. Diplodocids had pencil-shaped teeth. They could strip branches bare in seconds by raking leaves through their teeth.

What were meat eaters' teeth and claws like?

Meat eaters such as Allosaurus had long, curved, dagger-like teeth to kill and tear at prey. They had powerful jaws in their large heads and strong claws to grip their victims. Allosaurus could eat you up in two gulps!

Allosaurus

Is it true?
Some dinosaurs ate stones.

Yes. Plant eaters swallowed stones called gastroliths, to help grind down tough plant food inside their stomachs. Gastroliths were up to four inches across.

Amazing!
Carcharodontosaurus had a huge skull five feet across, with jaws full of teeth like a shark's. And yet some dinosaurs had no teeth at all! Gallimimus fed mainly on insects and tiny creatures it could swallow whole.

Tyrannosaurus rex

Tenontosaurus

? Whose teeth were as long as knives?

Tyrannosaurus rex, one of the last dinosaurs, was also one of the largest and fiercest meat eaters ever to live on Earth. Its ferocious teeth were six inches long. It used them to strip away flesh while it held its prey down with its feet.

Is it true?
Some dinosaurs were cannibals.

Yes. Two skeletons of Coelophysis have been found containing the bones of smaller Coelophysis. They had eaten the young animals as their last meal.

? What would kick out at its prey?

Deinonychus had an enormous slashing claw on each foot. It probably hunted and killed in packs, attacking its prey with a flying leap.

Baryonyx

Deinonychus

Amazing!

Baryonyx had large, curved claws that may have been used for hooking fish out of water. Its jaw was very similar to the jaws of modern fish-eating crocodiles.

? What had a 'terrible hand'?

Deinocheirus means 'terrible hand'. It had hands with long claws which must have been deadly, and arms ten feet long. Compared to this, T. rex's arms were tiny!

❓ What used its tongue in the same way as a giraffe?

Iguanodon used its long tongue to pull leaves into its mouth. On the 'thumb' of each hand it had a defensive spike. When this was first discovered, people thought it was a horn from its nose!

Iguanodon

Brachiosaurus

Is it true?
Most dinosaurs were peaceful, plant-eating creatures which never attacked anything.

Yes. Most dinosaurs were actually gentle animals, rather than monster killing machines like Tyrannosaurus Rex.

❓ Which dinosaurs traveled in groups?

Fossilized footprints from 80 million years ago tell us that Brachiosaurus traveled in herds, like most other plant-eating sauropods. It had huge nostrils, perhaps to smell with, to help cool it, or even to make a noise.

Amazing! Huge plant eaters had to eat a huge amount. A Brachiosaurus may have eaten a ton of vegetation a day. It must have spent its whole day walking, eating and producing waste!

Psittacosaurus

What had a beak like a parrot?

Psittacosaurus means 'parrot reptile'. With a narrow, parrot-like beak, strong jaws and sharp teeth, it was able to chew through very tough plants.

? Were huge plant eaters ever attacked?

The sheer size of many of these gentle giants must have put off many predators. Some like Apatosaurus had long claws to defend themselves in case they were attacked. They would rear up on their back legs and slash out at their enemies.

Heterodontosaurus

Ceratosaurus

Amazing! Plant eaters like Heterodontosaurus had fangs which they may have used to bite attackers. It was a small but strong dinosaur, well able to defend itself against meat eaters.

Is it true?
Scientists can tell how quickly dinosaurs could travel.

YES. By looking at their skeletons and measuring the distance between fossilized footprints, scientists can measure how quickly or slowly a dinosaur moved.

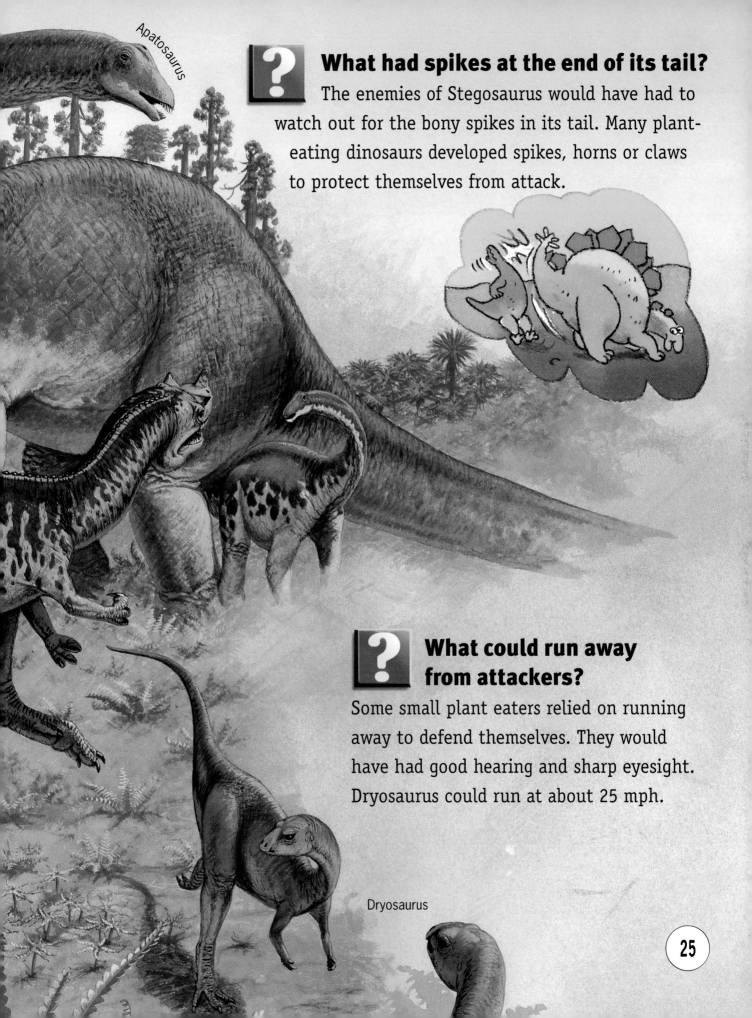

Apatosaurus

What had spikes at the end of its tail?

The enemies of Stegosaurus would have had to watch out for the bony spikes in its tail. Many plant-eating dinosaurs developed spikes, horns or claws to protect themselves from attack.

What could run away from attackers?

Some small plant eaters relied on running away to defend themselves. They would have had good hearing and sharp eyesight. Dryosaurus could run at about 25 mph.

Dryosaurus

25

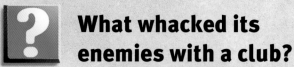

What whacked its enemies with a club?

The skull and body of Euoplocephalus were protected with bony plates, spines and spikes. It also had a huge club at the end of its tail. When attacked, it would swing this club at its enemy.

Is it true?
Stegosaurus used the plates on its back to defend itself.

NO. The plates may have looked frightening to enemies. But it's more likely that they helped control the animal's body temperature, so that it could warm up and cool down when it needed to.

Hylaeosaurus

Euoplocephalus

What wore armor to protect itself?

Many dinosaurs had a thick layer of bony skin which protected them like a suit of armor. Hylaeosaurus would lie low to the ground so that its attacker couldn't get under its armor.

Amazing! Another armored dinosaur, Huayangosaurus, had sharp spikes running from its shoulder to the middle of its tail. When it was attacked, it would point the spikes on its back at the enemy and lash out with its tail.

Tyrannosaurus rex

Triceratops

What had a horn like a rhinoceros?

Triceratops had three large horns, two over its eyes and one on its snout. Its neck and shoulders were protected by a frill of bone. There were many horned dinosaurs, most of which fed together in herds.

Which dinosaurs had 'trumpets'?

Many 'duck-billed' dinosaurs, like Parasaurolophus, had strange crests on their heads. The male's crest was much larger than the female's. It was hollow and connected to the nostrils. Perhaps these dinosaurs used their crests like trumpets, making sounds to show off to their mates or to threaten rival males.

Is it true?
Scientists were the first people to discover dinosaur tracks.

NO. Native Americans were using designs which included dinosaur footprints, long before dinosaur tracks were discovered by scientists.

Parasaurolophus

Pachycephalosaurus

Allosaurus

Diplodocus

? What used its tail as a whip?

Diplodocus was a huge, plant-eating dinosaur with an enormously long neck and tail. It could measure 88 feet from nose to tail. When it was attacked, it used its tail like a whip, lashing it from side to side.

? What used to fight with its head?

Male dinosaurs probably fought for territory and mates, like animals do today. Pachycephalosaurus had a skull with a dome of thick bone, like a crash helmet. This was probably to protect its brain during head-butting fights with rivals.

Did dinosaurs lay eggs?

Yes. Dinosaurs laid eggs, just as reptiles and birds do today. Scientists have found fossil eggs all over the world. Most are empty, but some eggs have been found with the fossil bones of baby dinosaurs inside.

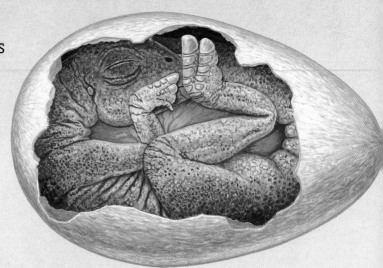

Centrosaurus

Did dinosaurs protect their young?

Horned dinosaurs like Centrosaurus lived in large family groups, like elephants. When threatened, the adults probably surrounded the young, making a frightening wall of horns.

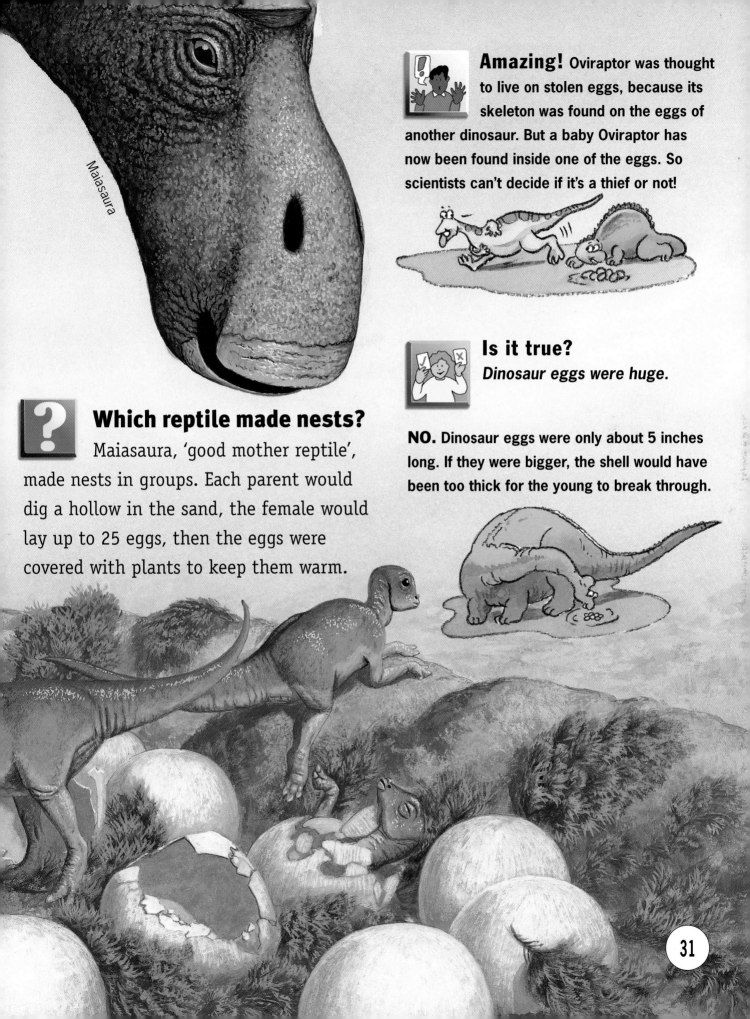

Maiasaura

Amazing! Oviraptor was thought to live on stolen eggs, because its skeleton was found on the eggs of another dinosaur. But a baby Oviraptor has now been found inside one of the eggs. So scientists can't decide if it's a thief or not!

Which reptile made nests?

Maiasaura, 'good mother reptile', made nests in groups. Each parent would dig a hollow in the sand, the female would lay up to 25 eggs, then the eggs were covered with plants to keep them warm.

Is it true?
Dinosaur eggs were huge.

NO. Dinosaur eggs were only about 5 inches long. If they were bigger, the shell would have been too thick for the young to break through.

31

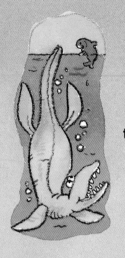

Amazing! The largest lizards ever were mosasaurs, huge reptiles that swam in the sea. They were real sea monsters – 32 feet long with huge mouths, and they looked like dragons! They probably ate anything they could catch.

Were there dinosaurs in the sea?

No. All dinosaurs lived on land, but there was a variety of strange reptiles that swam in the seas in dinosaur times. Ichthyosaurs were strong swimming reptiles that looked like dolphins and could breathe air. They probably hunted in packs, feeding on fish and squid.

Ammonite

Ichthyosaurs

Is it true?
The Loch Ness Monster exists.

WHO KNOWS? People who believe that there really is a monster in Loch Ness in Scotland, think it may well be a plesiosaur. What do you think?

❓ What was all neck?

Plesiosaurs were also swimming reptiles. They had four paddle-like limbs and a tail. Elasmosaurus was a long-necked plesiosaur. Its tiny head sat on an amazingly long neck that was half its total length of 42 feet.

Elasmosaurus

Liopleurodon

❓ What had a huge head?

Liopleurodon was one of the short-necked plesiosaurs. But its head was twelve feet long! It probably fed on shellfish and turtles, crunching them up with dagger-like teeth that were four inches long.

What was the earliest bird?

The earliest bird discovered was Archaeopteryx, which lived 150 million years ago. Birds are the dinosaurs' closest living relatives. Some scientists believe they evolved from dinosaurs such as Deinonychus, only smaller.

Archaeopteryx

Amazing!
Pterodaustro had a sieve in its beak so that it could strain fish from the water as it flew low over the sea.

Rhamphorhynchus

Were there flying dinosaurs?

The reptiles gliding through the air weren't dinosaurs but pterosaurs. The earliest pterosaurs were rhamphorhynchids which appeared about 200 million years ago.

? What were pterodactyls?

Pterodactyls, which means 'wing-finger', were pterosaurs. They were sleek and streamlined, and grew to huge sizes. They had crests on their heads, but no tail and no teeth. They appeared 150 million years ago and died out at the same time as the dinosaurs.

Pterodactylus

Is it true?
Quetzalcoatlus was bigger than a hang-glider.

YES. This huge pterodactyl was the biggest airborne animal that ever lived. It had a wingspan of up to 50 feet.

? Why did the dinosaurs disappear?

Some scientists think it was because a large meteorite hit Earth, or because huge volcanoes erupted and the climate changed. Movement of land and seas meant there were also fewer places for dinosaurs to live. It could be all of these reasons.

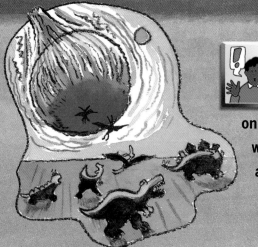

Amazing! A huge crater 110 miles across has been found on the seabed near Mexico. It was formed 65 million years ago. Could this be from a meteorite that wiped out the dinosaurs?

? Why would a meteorite wipe out the dinosaurs?

When the meteorite hit the surface of the Earth, there would have been a huge explosion. Dust would fill the air, blocking out the Sun's light for several months. Without the Sun vegetation would die, the plant eaters would die, and finally the large meat eaters would starve.

Zalambdalestes

Is it true?
People may have caused dinosaurs to become extinct.

NO. People and dinosaurs have never lived at the same time. There is a 60 million year gap between the last dinosaurs and the first human beings. So don't believe all the films that you see!

Did all the animals disappear?

No, although many other species died out along with the dinosaurs. These included pterosaurs and marine reptiles such as plesiosaurs. Most bigger animals became extinct. But smaller animals survived, and these creatures evolved in a world without the dinosaur.

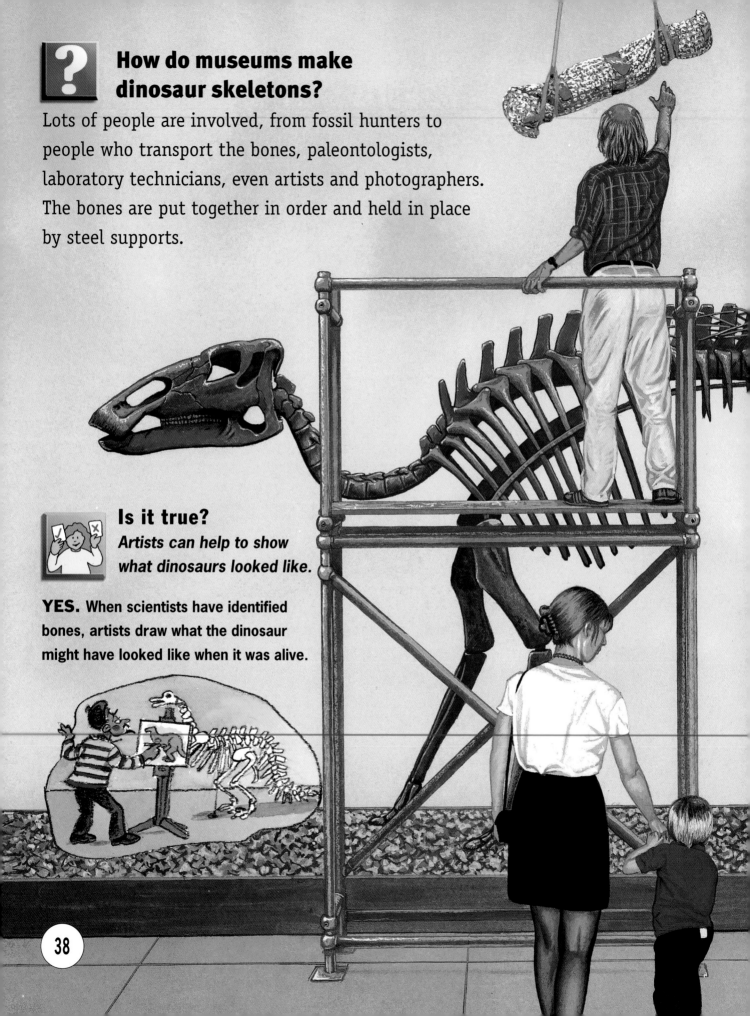

How do museums make dinosaur skeletons?

Lots of people are involved, from fossil hunters to people who transport the bones, paleontologists, laboratory technicians, even artists and photographers. The bones are put together in order and held in place by steel supports.

Is it true?
Artists can help to show what dinosaurs looked like.

YES. When scientists have identified bones, artists draw what the dinosaur might have looked like when it was alive.

Do museums use real bones?

No. Original fossils are too heavy and valuable. Instead scientists make copies from lightweight materials and keep the real bones safe.

Amazing! Scientists think that they might have found a missing link between birds and dinosaurs. Sinosauropteryx was a true dinosaur, but it had a feathery covering, and its feet had sharp pointed claws, much like a chicken's.

DINO DE TOUR

Sinosauropteryx

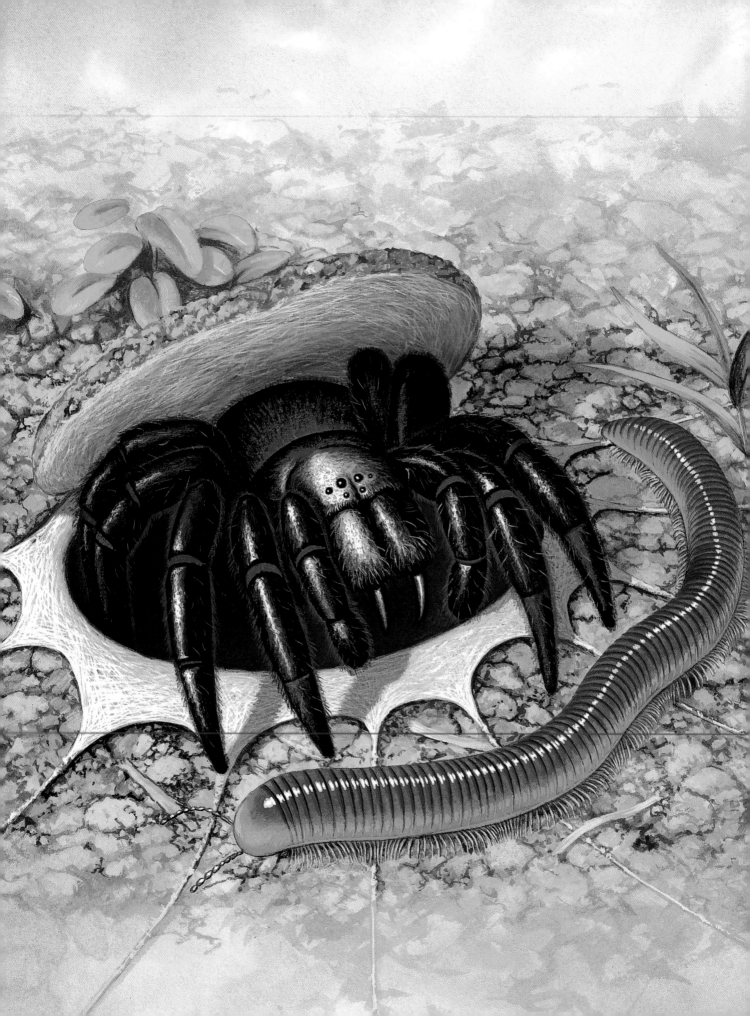

CHAPTER TWO

SPIDERS

AND OTHER CREEPY-CRAWLIES

Are spiders insects?

No. Spiders belong to a group called arachnids, which also includes scorpions, mites and ticks. Spiders all have eight legs, one pair more than insects. They have two body parts – a head and an abdomen – and most have eight simple eyes.

Is it true?
Spiders and insects have bones.

NO. Instead they all have a hard casing on the outside called an exoskeleton. This protects their soft insides like a suit of armor and gives them their shape. They have to replace this casing with a new one in order to grow.

Wolf spider

Amazing! There are creepy-crawlies living just about everywhere in the world, underwater, in caves, down deep holes and even on the tops of mountains. Most of the animals in the world are insects. They make up 85% of all known animal species and there are probably millions more waiting to be discovered!

Head

Thorax

Abdomen

? What makes an insect an insect?

Although they may look different from one another, every adult insect has six legs and three parts to its body. The head is at the front, the thorax in the middle and the abdomen at the back. Many insects have wings for flying and long feelers or antennae.

Pill bug

Snail

Earthworm

Centipede

Millipede

? What is a minibeast?

Creepy-crawlies can also be called minibeasts. You will find other kinds of minibeasts in this book which are related to spiders and insects, such as Pill bugs, slugs, snails, worms, centipedes and millipedes.

Which insect is as heavy as an apple?

The heaviest insect in the world is the African Goliath beetle. It weighs about four ounces and can be six inches long. It lives in rotten wood in tropical forests.

Goliath beetle

Is it true?
Some creepy-crawlies can live for 50 years.

YES. A queen termite may live to this ripe old age. But the life of an adult mayfly may be only a few hours long – just enough time for the mayfly to find a mate.

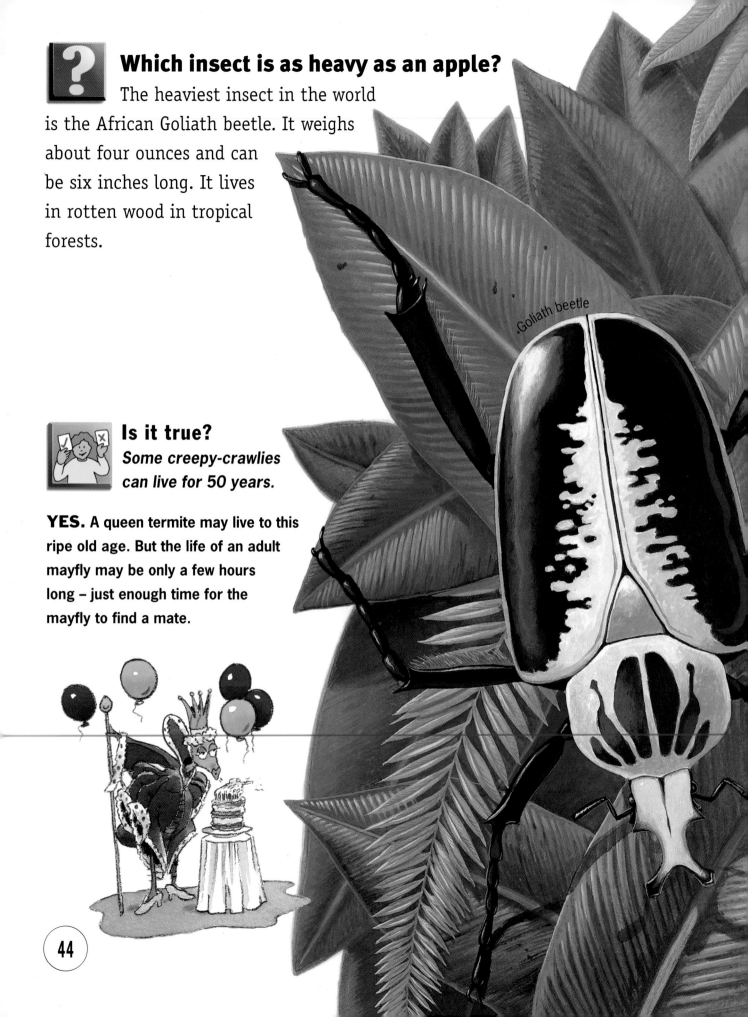

What grows up inside the eggs of other insects?

Fairy flies are actually tiny wasps, some of which have a wing span no bigger than a period! The female can lay up to 20 eggs inside the egg of another insect.

Fairy fly on insect eggs

Amazing! Fleas can jump 150 times their own body length. If humans could do this, we would be able to jump a third of a mile in the air! Fleas are wingless insects which suck blood from birds and mammals.

Rhinoceros beetle

Which is the strongest creature in the world?

Believe it or not, it's an insect. The rhinoceros beetle is able to move 850 times its own weight. Can you imagine trying to carry 850 people the same size as you?

45

Do spiders have teeth?

No, but they have fangs for stabbing prey and injecting it with poison and special juices. The victims turn to liquid inside so that the spider can then suck them up like soup!

Indian ornamental tarantula

Why do spiders spin webs?

Sticky webs can be a home and a trap to catch flying insects. But not all spiders make webs, and not all webs are the same. The ogre-eyed spider makes a web like a net. It hangs down holding the web, waiting to throw it over its prey.

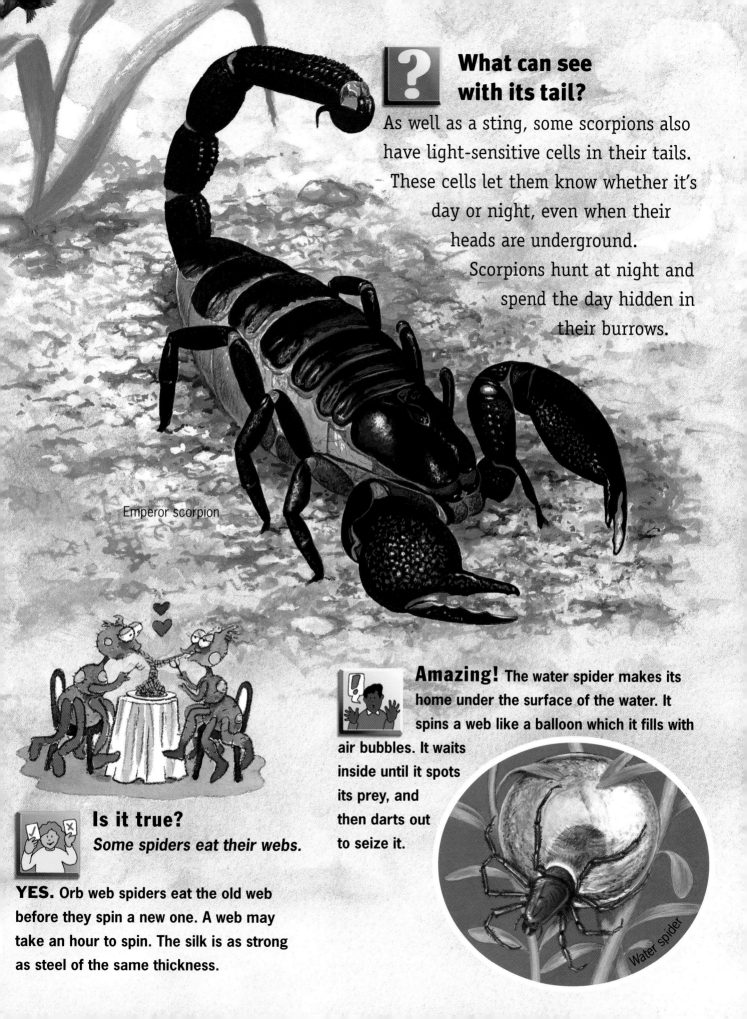

What can see with its tail?

As well as a sting, some scorpions also have light-sensitive cells in their tails. These cells let them know whether it's day or night, even when their heads are underground. Scorpions hunt at night and spend the day hidden in their burrows.

Emperor scorpion

Amazing! The water spider makes its home under the surface of the water. It spins a web like a balloon which it fills with air bubbles. It waits inside until it spots its prey, and then darts out to seize it.

Is it true?
Some spiders eat their webs.

YES. Orb web spiders eat the old web before they spin a new one. A web may take an hour to spin. The silk is as strong as steel of the same thickness.

Water spider

What can find its mate over a mile away in the dark?

Using its enormous feathery antennae, the male emperor moth can track down the scent of its mate even when she is far away. An insect's antennae are used for touching, smelling and tasting.

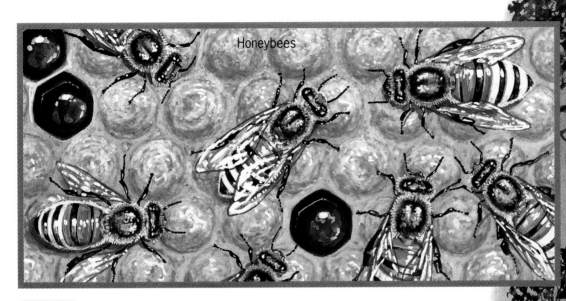
Honeybees

What does the waggle dance?

When a honeybee finds a good source of nectar, it flies back to the hive and does a special dance. The speed and direction of its movements tell the others where they can find the nectar.

Is it true?
All beetles can fly.

NO. Most have wings, but not all can fly. Beetles usually have two sets of wings. The first set is hard and strong, with the flying wings hidden beneath.

Eyes of a fly

Emperor moth

? Why is it so hard to swat a fly?

An insect's eye is made up of thousands of lenses. This means it sees a very different world from us. It's also much better at sensing any movement nearby.

Amazing! Dragonflies and some wasps and moths can fly as fast as 30 mph. Butterflies flap their wings 5 – 12 times per second, the hawkmoth 70 times, while some tiny flies can beat their wings 1,000 times each second!

49

What is the difference between a centipede and a millipede?

Centipedes and millipedes have long, bendy bodies made up of segments. A millipede has two pairs of legs on each segment, but centipedes have only one pair on each segment. Millipedes are plant eaters. Centipedes are meat eaters, hunting at night for tiny creatures which they attack with powerful poisonous jaws.

Centipede

Snail

What travels on one big foot?

Snails and slugs glide slowly along on one long muscular foot, leaving a trail of slime behind them. They prefer damp, dark places and are most active at night.

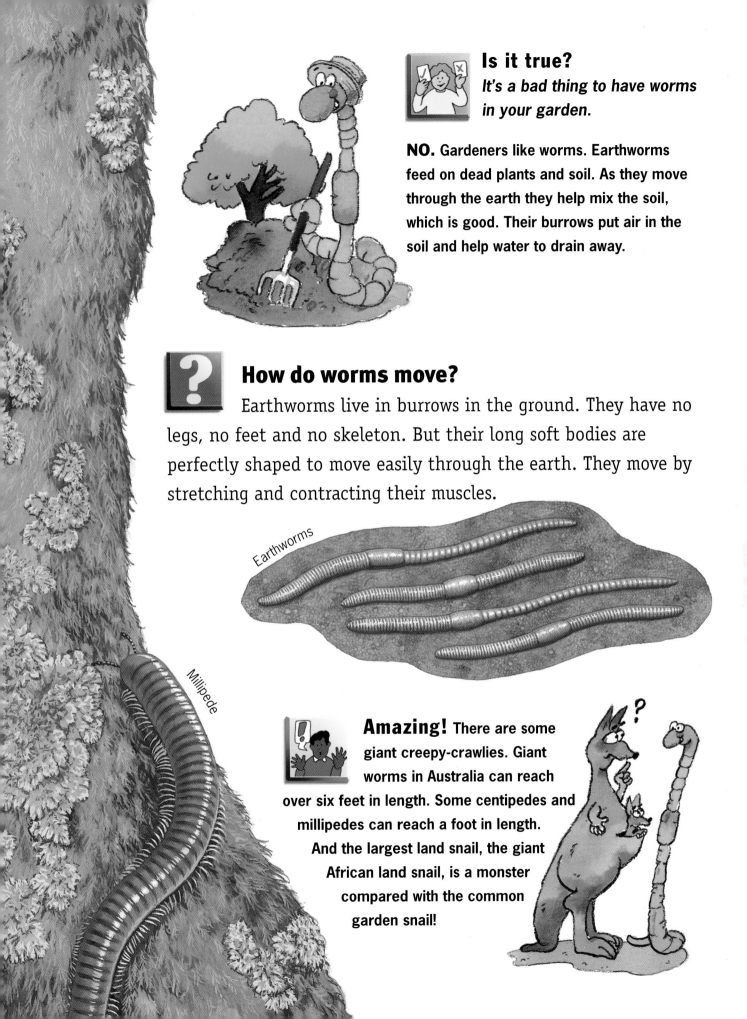

Is it true?
It's a bad thing to have worms in your garden.

NO. Gardeners like worms. Earthworms feed on dead plants and soil. As they move through the earth they help mix the soil, which is good. Their burrows put air in the soil and help water to drain away.

How do worms move?

Earthworms live in burrows in the ground. They have no legs, no feet and no skeleton. But their long soft bodies are perfectly shaped to move easily through the earth. They move by stretching and contracting their muscles.

Earthworms

Millipede

Amazing! There are some giant creepy-crawlies. Giant worms in Australia can reach over six feet in length. Some centipedes and millipedes can reach a foot in length. And the largest land snail, the giant African land snail, is a monster compared with the common garden snail!

? What is the difference between a moth and a butterfly?

Butterflies are often brightly colored. They fly during the day and their antennae have rounded ends. Moths have feathery antennae, and fly at night.

Croesus moth

Heliconid butterfly

? Which butterfly can fly thousands of miles?

The American monarch butterfly lives in the United States and Canada. When autumn approaches, thousands travel south to Florida, California and Mexico – a journey of over 1,800 miles.

Peacock butterfly

Is it true?
Butterflies and moths have scales.

YES. Butterflies and moths have four wings covered with tiny overlapping scales which shimmer in the light. These scales give them their bold patterns and beautiful colors.

Amazing! Before laying eggs, butterflies test food plants with their antennae and tongues to check that the leaves are suitable for their caterpillars. But some also stamp on the leaves, because butterflies, flies and honeybees have taste organs in their feet!

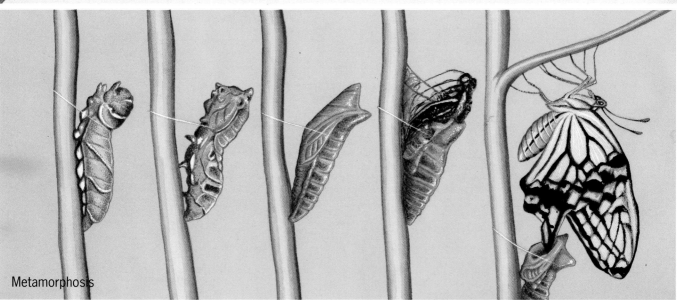

Metamorphosis

 ## How do caterpillars become butterflies?

When a caterpillar is fully grown, it turns into a pupa. Inside the pupa case the caterpillar's body breaks down and gradually becomes a butterfly. This change is called metamorphosis.

Tortoiseshell butterfly

Leaf insect

Stick insect

When is a plant not a plant?

When it's a stick or leaf insect! Stick and leaf insects are the same color and shape as the twigs and leaves on which they feed. During the day they sit very still. Predators leave them alone because they don't realize that they are insects.

Eyed hawkmoth

What frightens off enemies with its 'eyes'?

The eyed hawkmoth raises its front wings to show bold markings which look like large eyes. This fools enemies into thinking the moth is a much bigger animal than it really is.

54

Amazing! Beetles and pill bugs have an armor covering so tough that it is difficult to crush. This protects them from their enemies. Some pill bugs and millipedes roll into a ball like a hedgehog when they are threatened.

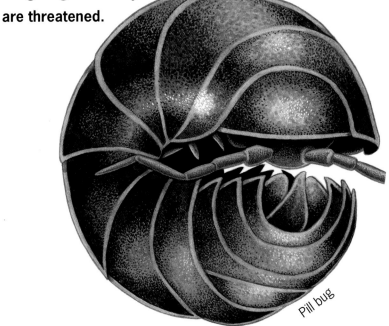

Pill bug

What pretends to be dead?

Click beetles lie on their backs as if they were dead to fool their enemies. Then they suddenly spring up in the air, twist and land on their feet, and run away!

Is it true?
Some spiders can change color.

YES. Crab spiders can change color to match the flowers they hide in. Lots of insects use camouflage to hide from their enemies. Invisible against the petals, the crab spider can pounce on unsuspecting bees, flies and butterflies as they visit the flower.

What uses a lasso to catch its prey?

The Bolas spider gives off a scent that attracts a particular moth. When the moth approaches, the spider swings out a line of silk with a sticky ball at the end. The ball sticks to the moth. The spider then hauls it in for supper.

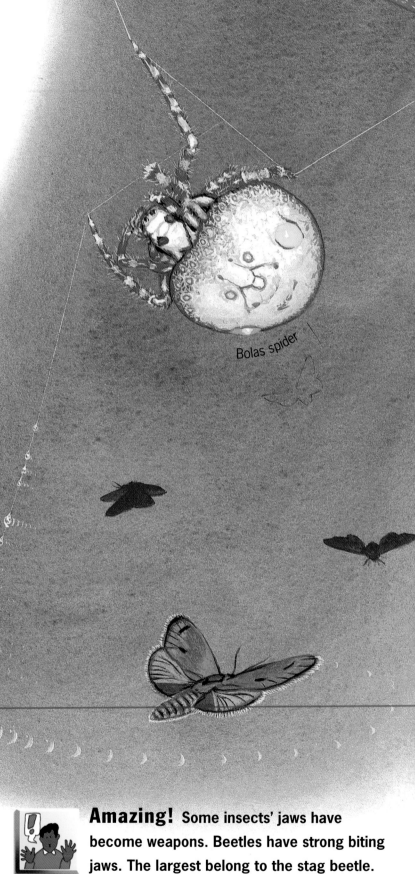

Bolas spider

Stag beetles

Amazing! Some insects' jaws have become weapons. Beetles have strong biting jaws. The largest belong to the stag beetle. They look like antlers and can be as long as the beetle's body. Beetles are the largest group of animals in the world, with over 300,000 kinds!

What is well equipped for battle?

Scorpions are protected with tough leathery armor. They also have many weapons – jagged jaws, huge pincers and a poisonous sting in their tail. Some have stings as venomous as a cobra's bite.

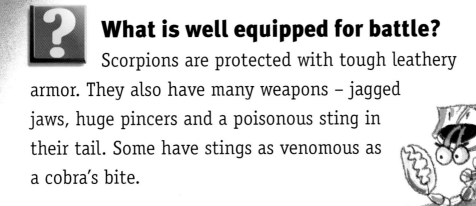

Is it true?

Ants can fire acid at their enemies.

YES. Wood ants fire a stinging acid from their abdomens. Ants can be dangerous little creatures. They can bite, and then squirt acid into the wound.

What spits at its prey?

All spiders produce silk, but only about half use silk to make webs or traps to catch prey. Other spiders hunt or pounce on their victims. The spitting spider lives up to its name. It catches prey by shooting sticky poisonous gum at it, fired through its fangs.

Spitting spider

57

What uses a trapdoor to catch its prey?

The trapdoor spider builds an
underground burrow, lined with silk
and covered with a hinged lid. It
lifts up the lid just a little,
peeps out and waits. When
prey approaches, it flips
open the trapdoor, leaps
out and attacks.

Trapdoor spider

Young dragonfly

What catches its victims with its lip?

Young dragonflies live in ponds and
streams. They catch tadpoles and small
fish using a special lower lip, which
shoots out to stab and hold prey.

Is it true?
Wasps will not attack spiders.

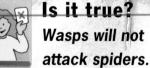

NO. The sting of the large spider wasp
can paralyze a spider three times its
size. The wasp then lays an
egg on the spider.
When the larva
hatches it eats the
spider alive.

Amazing! Spider webs come in many shapes and sizes. The purse web spider spins a long, tube-shaped web. The spider waits inside the web until an unsuspecting insect lands on the outside of the web. Then it bites through the silk and catches its prey.

Millipede

What creeps up on its prey?

The jumping spider stalks its prey like a cat, before suddenly pouncing. Even with eight eyes, most spiders are short-sighted, and rely on hairs on their legs to sense vibrations. But jumping spiders have excellent eyesight.

Jumping spider

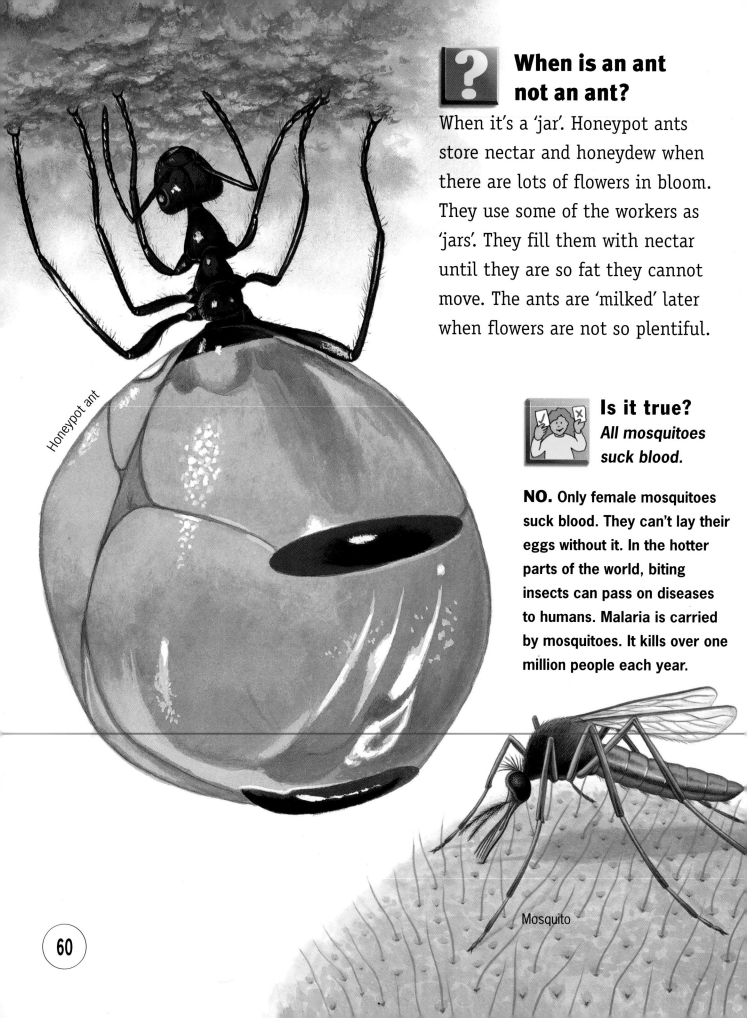

? When is an ant not an ant?

When it's a 'jar'. Honeypot ants store nectar and honeydew when there are lots of flowers in bloom. They use some of the workers as 'jars'. They fill them with nectar until they are so fat they cannot move. The ants are 'milked' later when flowers are not so plentiful.

Honeypot ant

Is it true?
All mosquitoes suck blood.

NO. Only female mosquitoes suck blood. They can't lay their eggs without it. In the hotter parts of the world, biting insects can pass on diseases to humans. Malaria is carried by mosquitoes. It kills over one million people each year.

Mosquito

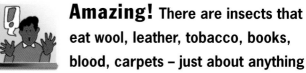

Amazing! There are insects that eat wool, leather, tobacco, books, blood, carpets – just about anything in the world you can think of. One insect, the male minotaur beetle, presents rabbit droppings to its mate as a tasty treat for her eggs!

What makes a bug a bug?

Bugs are a group of insects which all have a hollow needle-like tube that grows from their mouths. They use this 'beak' to suck up juices. Some live on the sap of plants. Others suck fluids from other insects and small animals.

Assassin bug feeding on a caterpillar

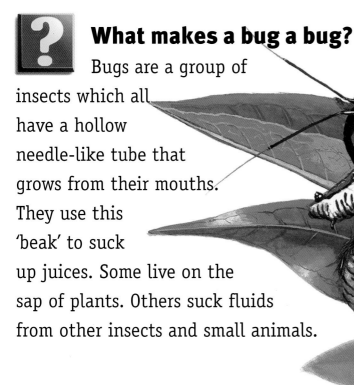

Which insect drinks with a straw?

Nearly all butterflies have a long hollow tongue called a proboscis which they use to suck up nectar. They keep their tongues curled up under their heads when they are not drinking.

Which insect lights up the sky when it's courting?

Male fireflies have special chemicals inside their bodies to make flashing light displays while searching for a mate. The females can't fly, but also send out light signals to help the males find them.

Firefly

Dancing spiders

Is it true?
Spiders dance to show off.

YES. Male spiders perform courtship dances in front of female spiders. When they find a mate, male spiders have to be careful. The female may be much larger. The dance helps the male persuade the female to mate with him, instead of eat him.

62

Why do crickets sing?
Male crickets and grasshoppers 'sing' to attract a mate. They rub their front wings together to make the noise, which is louder in hot weather.

Amazing!
Queen ants have wings at first. But after they've flown off and found a mate, they pull or rub their wings off. They no longer need them, because they are going to spend the rest of their lives producing eggs.

Praying mantis

Whose mate meets a horrid end?
The mantis eats its prey alive. For the female praying mantis, that includes her mate. She begins to eat the male while they are still mating.

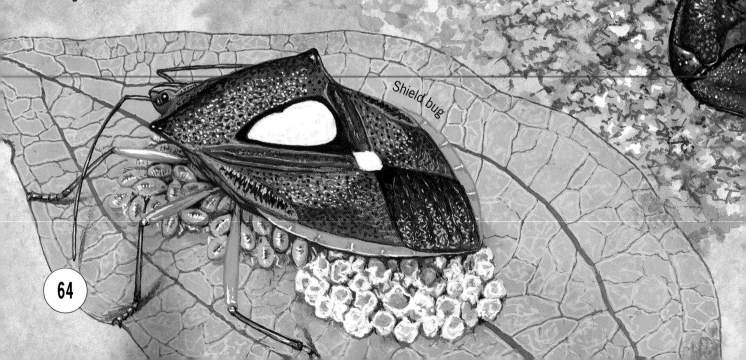

 Who makes a good mom?

 A female earwig looks after its eggs and young for several months. It keeps the eggs clean and warm, and feeds the young with food from its own stomach.

? What sits on its eggs until they hatch?

Some shield bugs protect their eggs by sitting on them. This keeps them safe from hungry predators. After hatching, they look after their young until they can move about.

Shield bug

64

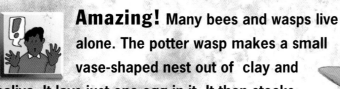

Amazing! Many bees and wasps live alone. The potter wasp makes a small vase-shaped nest out of clay and saliva. It lays just one egg in it. It then stocks the nest with food for the larva, seals it up and flies off to make another vase.

How do baby scorpions travel?

Unlike spiders, insects and other creepy-crawlies, scorpions give birth to live young. Some of them are cared for by the mother who carries the whole brood on her back. If one of the young falls off, she places her pincers on the ground so that it can climb back up again.

Potter wasp

Scorpion and young

Is it true?
A queen bee lays up to 3,500 eggs a day.

YES. Most creepy-crawlies produce large numbers of eggs. This makes sure that at least some survive to adulthood without getting eaten.

What lives in a skyscraper?

Termites build air-conditioned mounds that can be 20 feet tall. These nests contain a maze of tunnels and can be home to millions of termites. Each colony has a king, a queen and soldiers to guard it. In countries with a very wet climate, some termites build mounds with umbrella-shaped tops.

Termite mound

Is it true?
An ant's nest is full of different rooms.

YES. The nest is made up of many separate chambers, connected by a maze of tunnels. Some rooms are nurseries for the eggs and young, others are food cupboards and some are trash cans.

Queen termite

? What makes a nest in a tree?

Weaver ants make nests by pulling leaves together on a branch. They stick the leaf edges together using sticky silk which they gently squeeze from the ant larvae.

Weaver ants

Paper wasp

? What makes a paper nest?

Paper wasps build nests out of thin sheets of paper. They make the paper themselves by scraping wood from dead trees with their jaws and mixing it with saliva.

Amazing! Like ants and termites, honeybees live with thousands of others in colonies. They work together to find food, care for the young and protect the nest. The nest is made from waxy material which they shape into honeycomb. Honeybee nests are very strong and can last for 50 years.

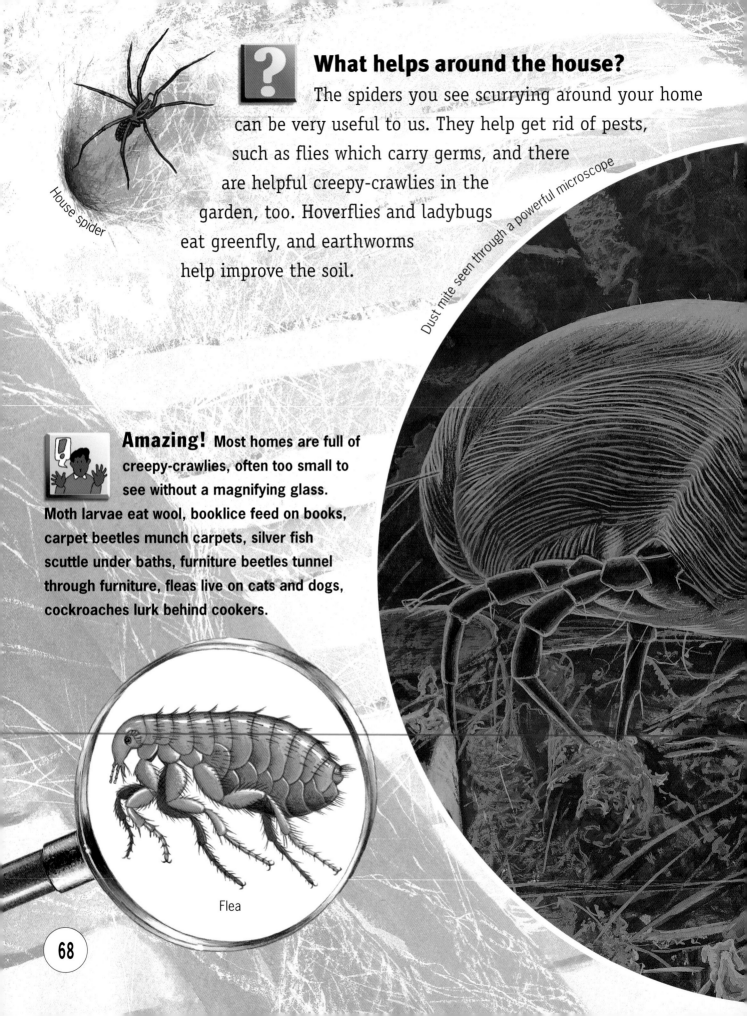

? What helps around the house?

The spiders you see scurrying around your home can be very useful to us. They help get rid of pests, such as flies which carry germs, and there are helpful creepy-crawlies in the garden, too. Hoverflies and ladybugs eat greenfly, and earthworms help improve the soil.

House spider

Dust mite seen through a powerful microscope

Amazing! Most homes are full of creepy-crawlies, often too small to see without a magnifying glass. Moth larvae eat wool, booklice feed on books, carpet beetles munch carpets, silver fish scuttle under baths, furniture beetles tunnel through furniture, fleas live on cats and dogs, cockroaches lurk behind cookers.

Flea

68

Who has been sleeping in my bed?

Dust mites are smaller than a period. They live all over the house, but they particularly like beds. Bedbugs are now quite rare, but in some countries they feed on sleeping people.

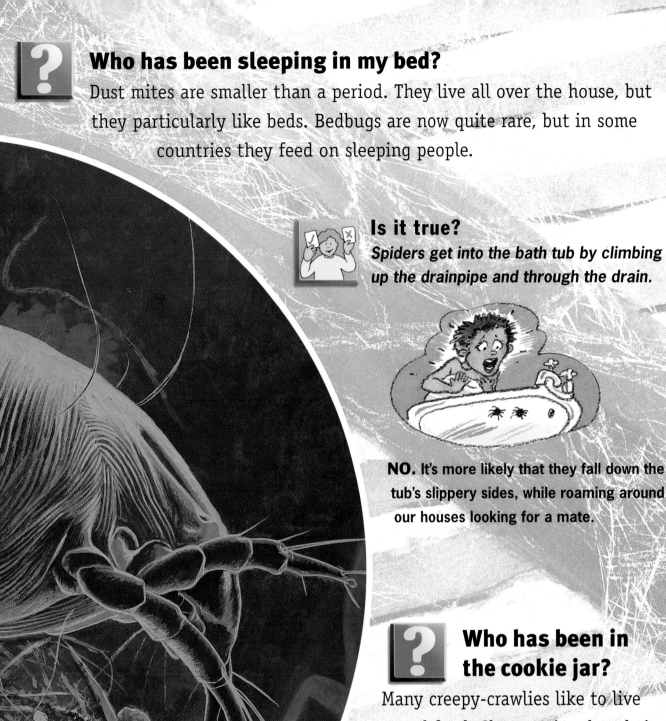

Is it true?

Spiders get into the bath tub by climbing up the drainpipe and through the drain.

NO. It's more likely that they fall down the tub's slippery sides, while roaming around our houses looking for a mate.

Who has been in the cookie jar?

Many creepy-crawlies like to live around food. Cheese mites lay their eggs on cheese. Spider beetles eat spices and sauce mixes. An old bag of flour may contain mites, caterpillars and beetles. Guess what the biscuit beetle prefers? Hard dry ones luckily, not stickie cookies.

CHAPTER THREE

SNAKES

AND OTHER REPTILES

❓ What are reptiles?

Reptiles are a group of animals that includes snakes, lizards, turtles, tortoises, alligators and crocodiles. They are all vertebrates (they have bones and skeletons inside their bodies), they breathe air and most of them live on land. Their skins are scaly to stop their bodies drying out.

Snake

Lizard

Amazing! Lizards love sunbathing. All reptiles are cold-blooded. They can't control their own body temperature but rely on the weather instead. Cold lizards are sluggish and slow. So they warm up in the sun, then scurry off hunting.

Turtle

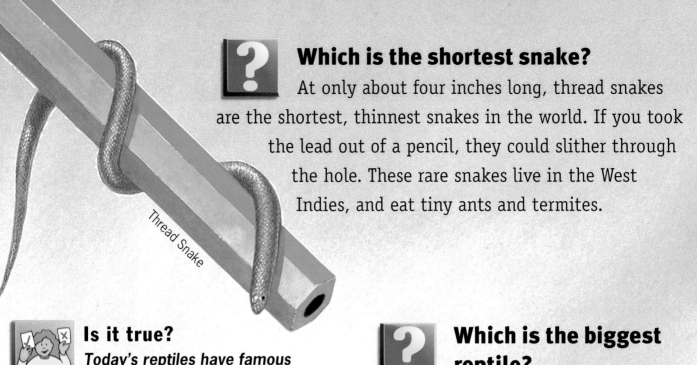

Which is the shortest snake?

At only about four inches long, thread snakes are the shortest, thinnest snakes in the world. If you took the lead out of a pencil, they could slither through the hole. These rare snakes live in the West Indies, and eat tiny ants and termites.

Thread Snake

Is it true?

Today's reptiles have famous relatives.

YES. The relatives of today's reptiles were the dinosaurs, which ruled the Earth for more than 200 million years. They suddenly died out about 65 million years ago.

Which is the biggest reptile?

The biggest reptiles alive today are saltwater crocodiles. They're usually about 13 feet long, but a gigantic crocodile killed in 1957 measured no less than 28 feet, and weighed more than two tons.

Saltwater crocodile

❓ Why do snakes shed their skin?

As a snake grows, its scaly skin gets too small. So the snake grows a new skin underneath, then slithers out of the old one, starting from the head and working down to the tail. A snake sheds its skin in one piece, several times a year.

Is it true?
You can tell a tortoise's age from its shell.

YES. A tortoise's shell is made of bone, covered in tough, horny plates. The shell protects the tortoise's body. But that's not all it's good for. Each year, the plates grow a new ring. Count these up, and you can use them to estimate the tortoise's age.

Which reptile has armor plating?

Alligators and crocodiles are covered in tough, horny scales, strengthened with bone. This waterproof armor stops their bodies drying out in the sun, and protects them from enemies.

Reticulated python

Amazing! Geckos have see-through eyelids. These are clear flaps of skin which protect their eyes from dust and dirt. A gecko can't blink to clean its eyelids. So it sticks out its tongue and licks them clean.

Which snake uses a rattle?

The rattle at the tip of a rattlesnake's tail is made of hollow scales, loosely linked together. If an enemy gets too close, the rattlesnake shakes its rattle, which makes a loud, angry buzzing sound to scare the attacker away. If this doesn't work, the rattlesnake coils itself up, then strikes with its poisonous fangs.

Which is the most poisonous land snake?

Some of the deadliest land snakes live in Australia. A drop of their poison could kill 250,000 mice. Other highly dangerous snakes include cobras, rattlesnakes, and taipans, which can grow to eleven feet long.

Which snake spits poison?

One type of cobra spits poison in its enemies' faces, blinding the victim! Spitting cobras have very good aims. They can hit a target more than six feet away.

Spitting cobra

Amazing! Fer-de-lance snakes have massive fangs and are deadly poisonous. They prey on rats and mice. Explorers claimed that local hunters in South America put these lethal snakes in tubes and fired them at their enemies.

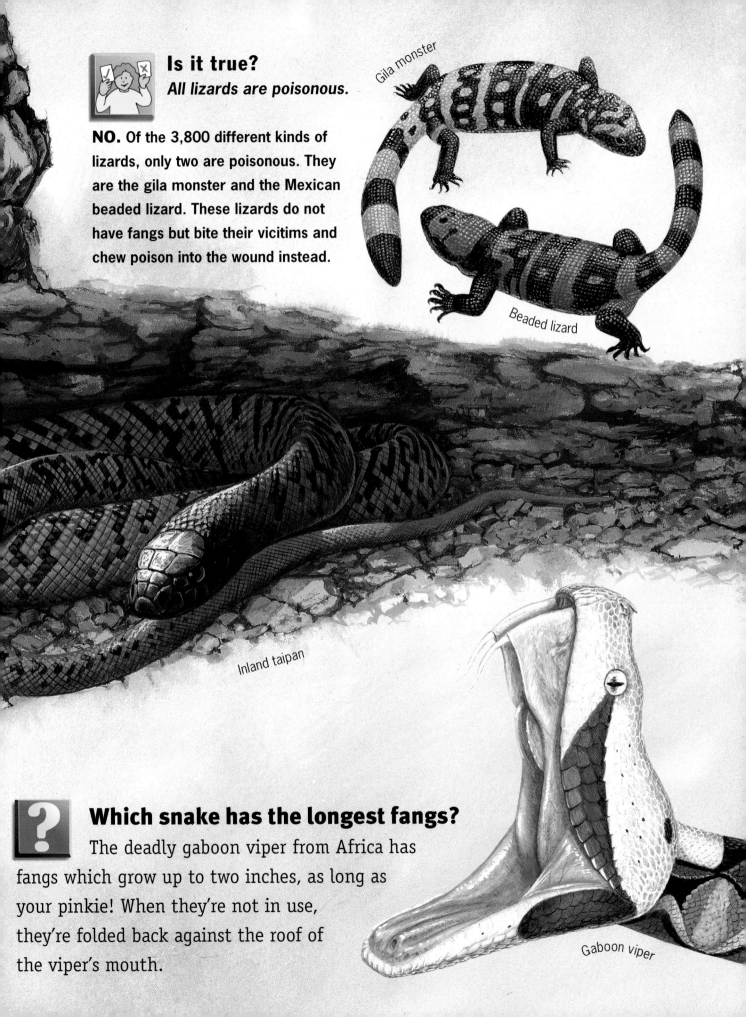

Is it true?

All lizards are poisonous.

NO. Of the 3,800 different kinds of lizards, only two are poisonous. They are the gila monster and the Mexican beaded lizard. These lizards do not have fangs but bite their vicitims and chew poison into the wound instead.

Gila monster

Beaded lizard

Inland taipan

Which snake has the longest fangs?

The deadly gaboon viper from Africa has fangs which grow up to two inches, as long as your pinkie! When they're not in use, they're folded back against the roof of the viper's mouth.

Gaboon viper

? What was the largest snake snack ever eaten?

The largest snack ever eaten by a snake was an impala antelope. It was devoured by an African rock python. The snake didn't chew its enormous meal into pieces. It swallowed the impala whole!

Rock python

Impala

? Which snake squeezes its prey to death?

A boa constrictor holds its prey in its teeth, then wraps its coils tightly around it. The snake does not crush its victim to death but squeezes it until it suffocates.

Is it true?
A snake can go for more than three years without food.

YES. It can take a snake weeks to digest a large meal. So they don't need to eat very often. A pit viper once survived without food for three years, three months - a world record.

Why do snakes have elastic jaws?

A snake has sharp, backward-pointing teeth. Its teeth are good at holding food but can't bite it into chunks. Instead, snakes swallow their prey whole. Snakes have amazingly stretchy jaws, with elastic-like hinges between their jawbones. This means they can open their mouths very wide, to swallow food larger than the size of their heads, such as eggs.

Amazing! There are many scary stories of snakes swallowing people. But only a few of them are true. In 1979, a young boy in South Africa was seized by a 14 feet-long African rock python. His friends ran off to get help. When they came back about 20 minutes later, the snake had swallowed the boy whole.

79

Is it true?

Crocodiles don't like the taste of people.

NO. Crocodiles do find people tasty, especially if they're hungry. It's estimated that saltwater crocodiles kill and eat up to 2,000 people each year.

Which lizard uses its tongue as a catapult?

A chameleon has a very long, sticky tongue. When it spots a tasty insect, it shoots out its tongue like a catapult, catches the insect and pulls it in. All in a split second.

Chameleon

Amazing! Alligators and crocodiles can snap their ferocious jaws shut with terrible force, but the muscles for opening their mouths up again are surprisingly weak. All you need to keep a crocodile's mouth shut is an elastic band. But keep your fingers away from those sharp, pointed teeth!

❓ Which lizard stores food in its tail?

The gila monster lives in the desert. It feeds on insects, birds' eggs and rodents. When there's plenty of food, it eats more than it needs and stores some as fat in its tail. It lives off this store when food is short.

Gila monster

Marine iguana

❓ Which lizard loves seaweed?

The marine iguana lives on the Galapagos Islands. It loves eating seaweed. At low tide, it dives into the water and clings on to a weed-covered rock with its claws. It tears off the seaweed with its mouth.

? Which snake pretends to be poisonous?

The milk snake lives in the rainforests of Central America. It's shy, secretive and harmless, but its bright bands of red, yellow and black make it look like the deadly coral snake. Its enemies think the milk snake is equally poisonous, and so leave it well alone.

Coral snake

Milk snake

Is it true?
Some snakes mimic vines.

YES. The African vine snake hangs down from tree branches, looking just like a harmless vine. There's a nasty suprise for any bird that perches on it. It suddenly snatches the bird and swallows it down.

Vine snake

? Which snake looks like sand?

Many desert snakes are perfectly camouflaged to look like sand. The horned viper lies in the sand with just its 'horns' showing. When a tasty desert rat passes by, the snake pounces.

Amazing! Chameleons are brilliant at changing color. They can go from almost white to black in minutes. They change color to blend in with their surroundings and to show they are feeling angry or frightened.

Leaf-tailed gecko

? Where do leaf-tailed geckos hide?

Pressed upside down against a tree trunk, the leaf-tailed gecko is almost impossible to see. Its body and tail are dappled brown and green to look exactly like the bark of the tree. The ragged fringe of scales around its body and legs hides its outline. It lives on the island of Madagascar.

83

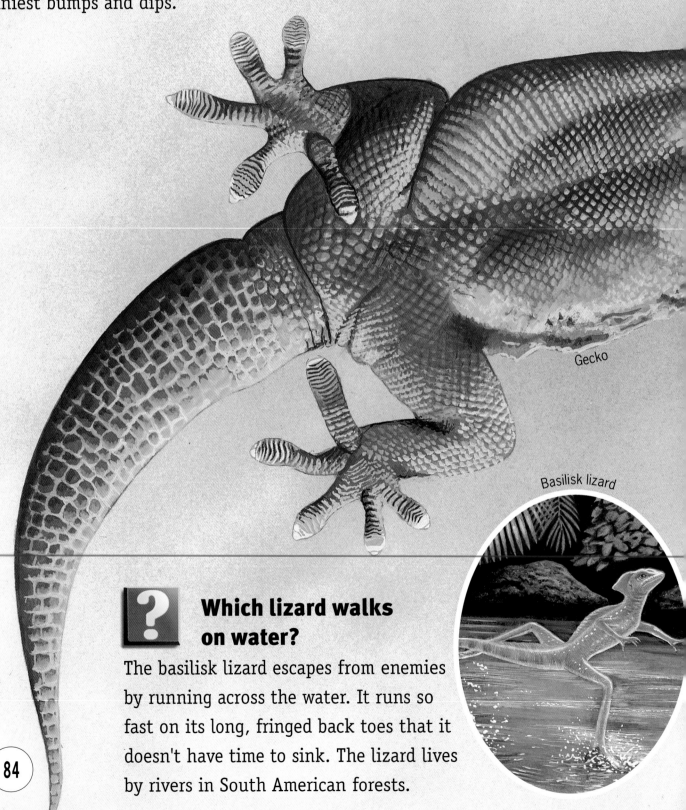

Who walks upside down?

Geckos can run up smooth walls and walk upside down across ceilings. They have special suction pads on their feet which allow them to cling on. The pads are covered in thousands of tiny hairs which help the geckos to grip the tiniest bumps and dips.

Gecko

Basilisk lizard

Which lizard walks on water?

The basilisk lizard escapes from enemies by running across the water. It runs so fast on its long, fringed back toes that it doesn't have time to sink. The lizard lives by rivers in South American forests.

Amazing! Tortoises are real slow pokes. Their heavy shells weigh them down so much that they move about very slowly, or not at all. Most tortoises lumber along at speeds of less than 0.3 mph, even when they're hungry.

Which lizard runs the fastest?

The speediest lizard is the spiny-tailed iguana. It can speed along at almost 22 mph, about the same speed as a champion sprinter. In an experiment, a racetrack was set up and the lizards were timed with the same devices used at the Olympic Games.

Is it true?
Dragons can fly.

YES. Flying dragons are small lizards. To travel through the trees, they take to the air. They glide from branch to branch on special 'wings'. These are flaps of skin stretched over very long ribs which stick out from the sides of their body.

Flying dragon

85

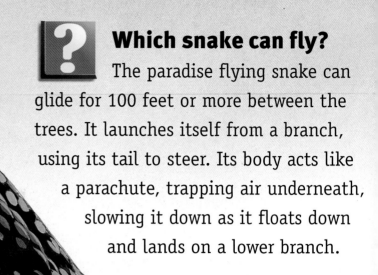

Which snake can fly?

The paradise flying snake can glide for 100 feet or more between the trees. It launches itself from a branch, using its tail to steer. Its body acts like a parachute, trapping air underneath, slowing it down as it floats down and lands on a lower branch.

Amazing!

The fastest land snake is the deadly black mamba. There are tales of them overtaking galloping horses. This isn't true but these speedy snakes can race along at about 12 mph.

Black mamba

Can snakes climb trees?

Many snakes slither through the trees, after birds and insects to eat. They are excellent climbers, with rough scales on the underside of their bodies to help them grip slippery branches.

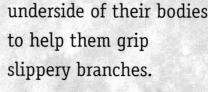

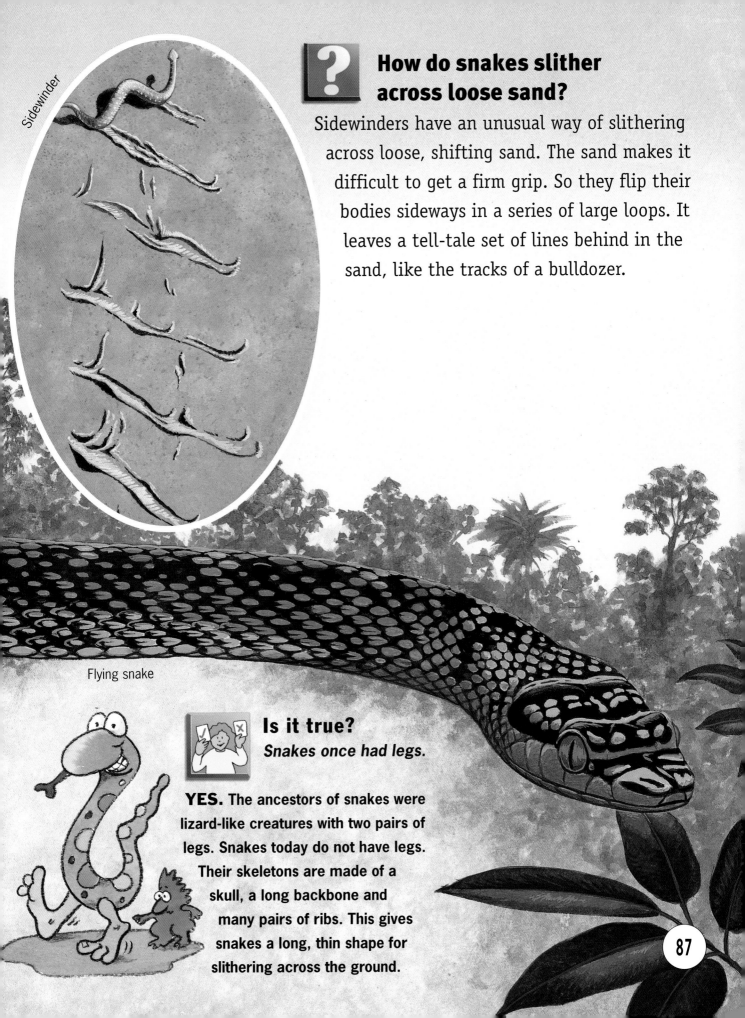

Sidewinder

How do snakes slither across loose sand?

Sidewinders have an unusual way of slithering across loose, shifting sand. The sand makes it difficult to get a firm grip. So they flip their bodies sideways in a series of large loops. It leaves a tell-tale set of lines behind in the sand, like the tracks of a bulldozer.

Flying snake

Is it true?
Snakes once had legs.

YES. The ancestors of snakes were lizard-like creatures with two pairs of legs. Snakes today do not have legs. Their skeletons are made of a skull, a long backbone and many pairs of ribs. This gives snakes a long, thin shape for slithering across the ground.

Do all reptiles lay eggs?

Most reptiles lay eggs with tough shells to protect the babies inside. But some types of snakes and lizards give birth to live young. When they are born, they look like miniature versions of their parents.

Which reptile eats its babies?

Large alligators only eat smaller ones during food shortages, and sometimes that includes their own young! When alligator babies hatch, their mother picks them up in her mouth and carries them safely to the water.

Alligator and young

88

Amazing! Most snakes don't look after their eggs at all. But pythons are caring parents. The females coil their bodies around their eggs to guard them from attack. They also shiver and shake their coils slightly to keep the eggs warm.

Green tree python

Green turtle

 ## Which babies are born on a beach?

Sea turtles come ashore to lay their eggs in nests on the beach. The female covers them with sand, then goes back to the sea. The eggs take about a month to hatch.

Is it true?
Baby green tree pythons are green.

NO. Baby green tree pythons are yellow or red. They don't change color to green until they're two years old.

Some geckos bark like dogs.

YES. The barking gecko and the tokay gecko both bark like dogs. They use their loud voices to attract mates or defend their territory.

Spectacled cobra

How well can snakes hear?

Snakes can't hear at all. They have no outer ears for detecting sounds. Instead, they pick up vibrations in the ground through their bodies. Snake charmers make it look as if a snake is dancing to the sound of music. But the snake is actually following the movement of the snake charmer's pipe with its eyes, ready to attack.

Amazing! Crocodiles and alligators are very noisy. They cough, hiss and bellow to attract mates and keep in touch with their group. The American alligator roars like a lion. It can be heard about 500 feet away.

How do snakes smell with their tongues?

Snakes don't smell things through their noses like we do. They pick up smell with their tongues, which they flick in and out. They can recognize different smells with the Jacobson's organ in the roof of the mouth.

Jacobson's organ

Which reptile can look in two ways at once?

Chameleons can move each of their large, bulging eyes on its own. This means they can look in two ways at once. When they're hunting, one eye can look out for tasty insects to eat. The other can watch out for hungry enemies.

Chameleon

Blue-tongued skink

 Why do skinks stick out their tongues?

When a blue-tongued skink is threatened, it simply sticks out its bright blue tongue. Its enemies quickly run away. Skinks are types of lizards. The biggest skinks grow to over two feet, as long as your arm.

Hognosed snake

 Is it true?
Hognosed snakes imitate rattlesnakes.

YES. A hognosed snake has an ingenious way of protecting itself from enemies. It pretends to be a deadly poisonous rattlesnake. It rubs its tail against its body to make a sinister rattling sound. If this fails, the snake rolls on to its back and pretends to be dead.

Frilled lizard

 Which turtle smells terrible?

The tiny stinkpot turtle lives in North America. It spends most of its time in slow-moving streams. As well as its shell, the turtle has a secret weapon to use against its enemies. It gives off a truly terrible smell!

? How do frilled lizards scare off attackers?

If a frilled lizard is chased into a corner, it puts on a dramatic show. It faces its attacker, with mouth wide open, and fans out the huge frill of skin around its neck. Then it sways from side to side, while hissing menacingly. It might look frightening, but in fact it's a fairly harmless lizard.

Amazing!

If its tail is grabbed by an enemy, a lizard simply runs off and leaves its tail behind. The tail breaks off at a special weak spot between the tail bones. Luckily, the lizard can grow a brand-new tail, although it is often shorter than the old one.

Amazing! Water skinks have anti-freeze in their blood. Special chemicals stop their blood freezing even if the temperature falls below zero. This means that the skinks can come out of hibernation when there is still snow on the ground. Water skinks live in the mountains of eastern Australia.

? How does a horned lizard warn off enemies?

The horned lizard is an odd-looking reptile, covered in prickly spines. If it's attacked, it has a weird way of defending itself. It sprays blood from its eyes. This may fool its enemy into thinking it's wounded and leaving it alone.

Black rattlesnake

Horned lizard

Which turtle uses its neck as a snorkel?

The matamata turtle lives in slow-moving rivers in South America. It lurks on the riverbed, with its mouth wide open, waiting to snap up passing prey. It uses its long neck as a snorkel to hold its nostrils out of the water. In this way, it can breathe without having to swim up to the surface.

Matamata turtle

Is it true?
Crocodiles cry real tears.

YES. Saltwater crocodiles look as if they are crying. But it's not because they are sad. They cry to get rid of extra salt which they take in with their food. People use the saying 'crocodile tears' to mean pretend tears.

Armadillo lizard

Which lizard looks like an armadillo?

The armadillo lizard has tough, armor-like skin on its head and back, just like a real armadillo. To escape from enemies, it hides in a crack in the rock, or it curls up into a tight, scaly ball to protect its soft stomach.

 Amazing! The lizard-like tuatara is the only survivor of a group of reptiles that lived in the time of the dinosaurs. By 65 million years ago, the rest of the group had died out. Only the tuatara was left. Tuataras are only found in New Zealand. Their name means 'spiny backed' in the local Maori language.

Reticulated python

 Which is the longest snake?

The giant reticulated python can measure up to 33 feet long. That's longer than six bicycles standing end to end. No snake could grow longer than 50 feet. It would be too heavy to move.

Komodo dragon

Sea snakes are the most poisonous snakes.

YES. All sea snakes are poisonous. One of the most poisonous of all is the banded sea snake from around Australia. Its venom is many times stronger than the deadliest land snake. Luckily, this snake rarely bites human beings.

Sea snake

Which is the biggest lizard?

The Komodo dragon is the world's largest lizard. Males can grow to more than nine feet long and weigh more than 330 pounds. These record-breaking reptiles live on a few islands in Indonesia. They are meat-eaters and can swallow deer and pigs whole!

Which reptile lives the longest?

Tortoises live longer than any other animals on land. The oldest tortoise known was a Marion's tortoise from the Seychelles. When it died in 1918, it was thought to be over 150 years old.

97

? Which is the smallest lizard?

A little gecko from the Caribbean is the world's smallest lizard. This tiny reptile is only just over an inch long. That's about as long as your thumb.

British Virgin Island gecko

? Which is the largest turtle?

The leatherback turtle is about the size of a small car. This giant reptile can grow almost ten feet long, from its head to the tip of its tail. It measures nearly ten feet across its front flippers. It can weigh almost a ton.

Leatherback turtle

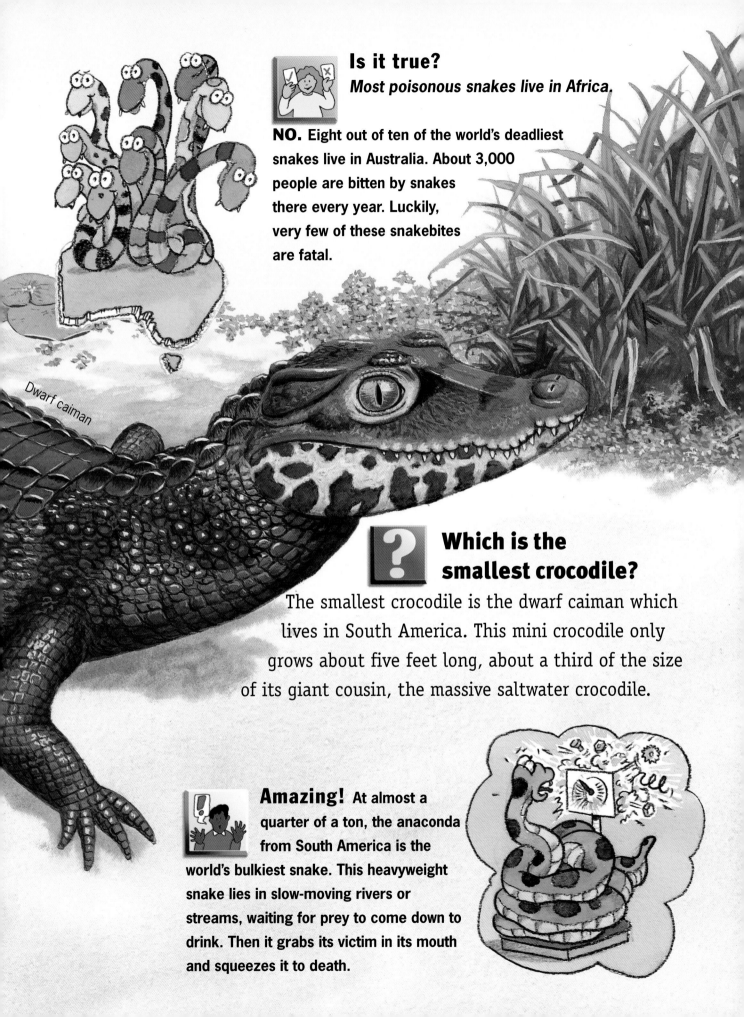

Is it true?
Most poisonous snakes live in Africa.

NO. Eight out of ten of the world's deadliest snakes live in Australia. About 3,000 people are bitten by snakes there every year. Luckily, very few of these snakebites are fatal.

Dwarf caiman

Which is the smallest crocodile?

The smallest crocodile is the dwarf caiman which lives in South America. This mini crocodile only grows about five feet long, about a third of the size of its giant cousin, the massive saltwater crocodile.

Amazing! At almost a quarter of a ton, the anaconda from South America is the world's bulkiest snake. This heavyweight snake lies in slow-moving rivers or streams, waiting for prey to come down to drink. Then it grabs its victim in its mouth and squeezes it to death.

CHAPTER FOUR

SHARKS

AND OTHER DANGEROUS FISH

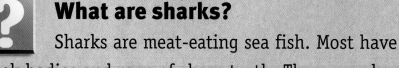

? What are sharks?

Sharks are meat-eating sea fish. Most have sleek bodies and rows of sharp teeth. There are about 375 types, of different shapes and sizes, living in different parts of the world. The dwarf shark is only four inches long, while the whale shark, the biggest of all fish, is 50 feet.

Hammerhead shark

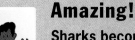 **Amazing!**
Sharks become sluggish in cool water, and so most prefer to live in warm seas. But the huge Greenland shark, 20 feet long, enjoys icy water. It lives in the North Atlantic, hunting for fish and seals beneath the pack ice.

Megalodon tooth

? How old are sharks?

Fossils show that sharks appeared more than 350 million years ago, long before the dinosaurs. Megalodon was a huge shark which hunted large prey and probably ate shellfish too. Its teeth were about three inches long.

Whale shark

Is it true?
All sharks are dangerous.

NO. In the order of dangerous sharks, the great white is most feared by people. But most sharks are harmless to us, and will only attack if they are disturbed. Other dangerous sharks include the tiger shark, mako, bronze and black-tipped whalers, and hammerhead.

Manta ray

Basking shark

Are sharks different from other fish?

Sharks, and their relatives the skates and rays, have skeletons made of rubbery cartilage. Other fish have skeletons made of bone. A shark's gill slits are not covered like other fish, but are in a row behind its head.

103

How fast can a shark swim?

Sharks such as the mako shark are perfect swimming machines, capable of speeds of up to 45 mph. Their sleek shape means they can move quickly through the water and turn at speed.

Is it true?
Sharks never have a break.

NO. Sharks living near the surface must swim all their lives to avoid sinking. But others like the nurse shark spend most of their time motionless on the seabed. Nurse sharks can pump water over their gills and so they don't need to keep moving.

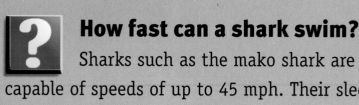

Gray reef shark

Why are sharks darker on top?

Sharks which swim near the surface are dark on top and paler on their undersides. This means they are difficult to see from above or below as they hunt for prey.

Blue shark

Amazing! Most sharks drown if they stop swimming, as no oxygen-rich water is passing over their gills. They also sink. They do not have a swim bladder like other fish. They have a huge oily liver instead, which helps to keep them afloat.

How do sharks breathe?

Like all fish, sharks extract oxygen from the water using their gills. Water enters their mouths, and oxygen is absorbed as the water passes over the red, feathery, blood-filled gills. Most sharks keep moving all the time in order to get a constant supply of oxygen.

Water leaves through gill slits

Oxygen-rich water enters mouth

Sand tiger shark

? Do sharks have the same senses as us?

Sharks have the five senses of sight, smell, taste, hearing and touch. They also have one more. Sensitive cells on their snouts allow them to pick up tiny electrical signals from other animals.

Reef sharks

? How do sharks know when an animal is struggling nearby?

Sharks can tell that there are animals in their area, even when there is no blood to smell. A sensitive 'lateral line' along their bodies allows them to feel ripples in the water from any struggling animal or person.

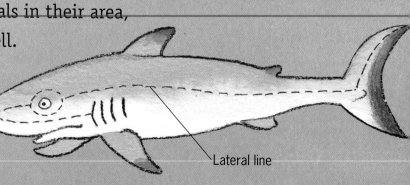

Lateral line

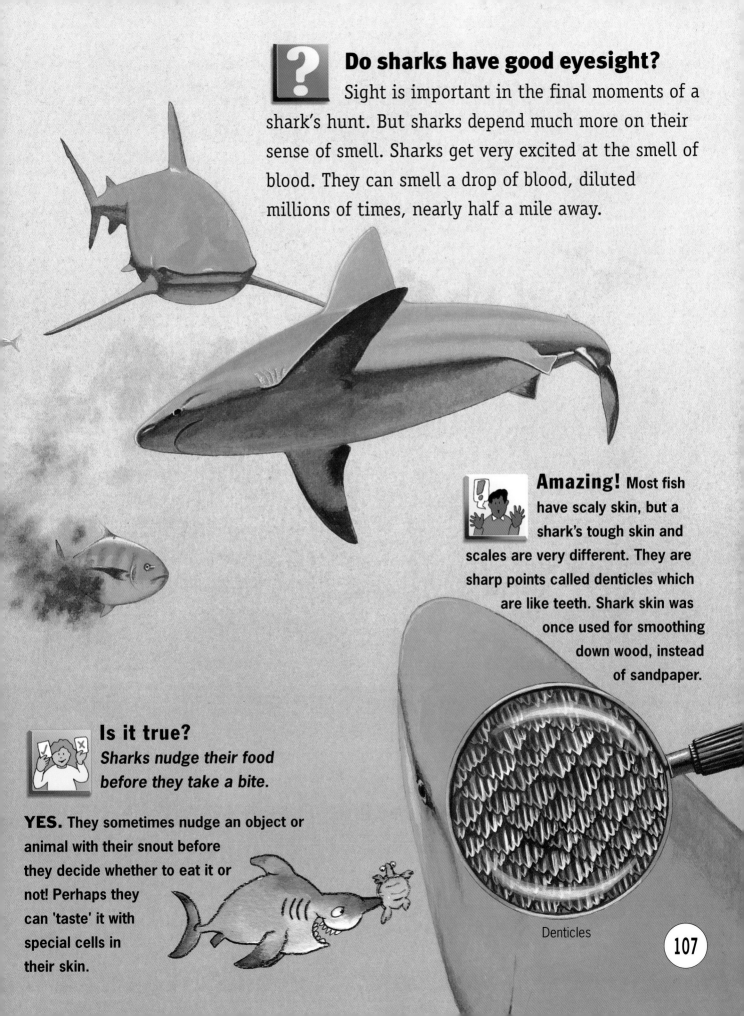

Do sharks have good eyesight?

Sight is important in the final moments of a shark's hunt. But sharks depend much more on their sense of smell. Sharks get very excited at the smell of blood. They can smell a drop of blood, diluted millions of times, nearly half a mile away.

Amazing! Most fish have scaly skin, but a shark's tough skin and scales are very different. They are sharp points called denticles which are like teeth. Shark skin was once used for smoothing down wood, instead of sandpaper.

Is it true?
Sharks nudge their food before they take a bite.

YES. They sometimes nudge an object or animal with their snout before they decide whether to eat it or not! Perhaps they can 'taste' it with special cells in their skin.

Denticles

What eats its unborn brothers and sisters?

Some sharks give birth to only a few baby sharks, or pups. This is because the first pups to develop eat the other eggs and embryos inside the mother. Often only one mako pup survives because it eats all the others.

Adult and young mako

Amazing! Some sharks take nine months to develop inside the mother, as long as a human baby. But the spiny dogfish takes 24 months! Young sharks are then on their own, even though it may be years before they are ready for the open sea.

108

Do sharks lay eggs?

In most sharks, fertilized eggs develop inside the female's body. But some sharks lay eggs and then swim away, leaving the eggs to develop on their own. Dogfish lay eggs in leathery cases, which are called 'mermaid's purses'.

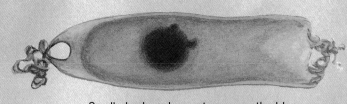
Swell shark embryo at one-month-old

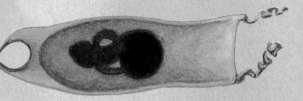
Three-month-old embryo

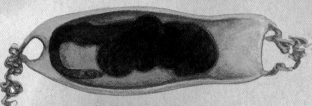
Seven-month-old embryo

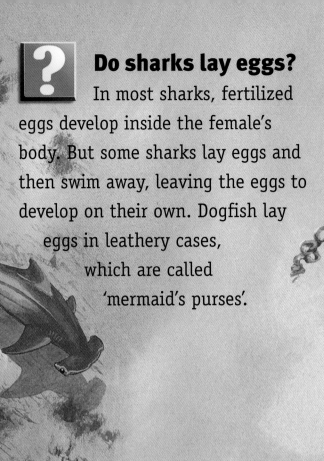
Hammerhead shark pups

Is it true?
Sharks never eat their own young.

NO. Some sharks give birth, and then if they come across their pup later in the day they will eat it!

What gives birth to lots of pups?

As many as 40 hammerhead shark pups may be born in one litter. They develop in a similar way to human babies, inside their mother's body.

Amazing!
Sometimes when a shark feeds, others join in. They get excited at the blood and movement around them, and seem to go crazy, biting, twisting and turning wildly in a 'feeding frenzy'.

❓ What is known as the trash can of the sea?

Tiger sharks will eat anything. They are not put off by a crunchy turtle shell, or a stinging jellyfish, or even a poisonous snake. They will happily munch dead animals that have been washed out to sea, old boots, papers, tin cans, plastic bags – and even people!

Tiger shark

How many teeth do sharks have?

Sharks are born with jaws full of teeth, neatly arranged in rows. They grow teeth all their lives. When front ones wear out or are lost, they're replaced by new teeth behind.

Sand tiger shark

Is it true?

A shark's teeth last for months.

NO. Once a rear tooth has moved to the front row, it may drop out, snap off or be worn away in as little as two weeks.

Do all sharks have the same teeth?

The shape and size depend on a shark's food. For example, the great white has slicing teeth for tearing off chunks of seal or dolphin. The Port Jackson has sharp front teeth to hold shellfish, and blunt back teeth to crush them.

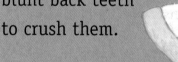

Tiger shark tooth

Mako tooth

Great white shark tooth

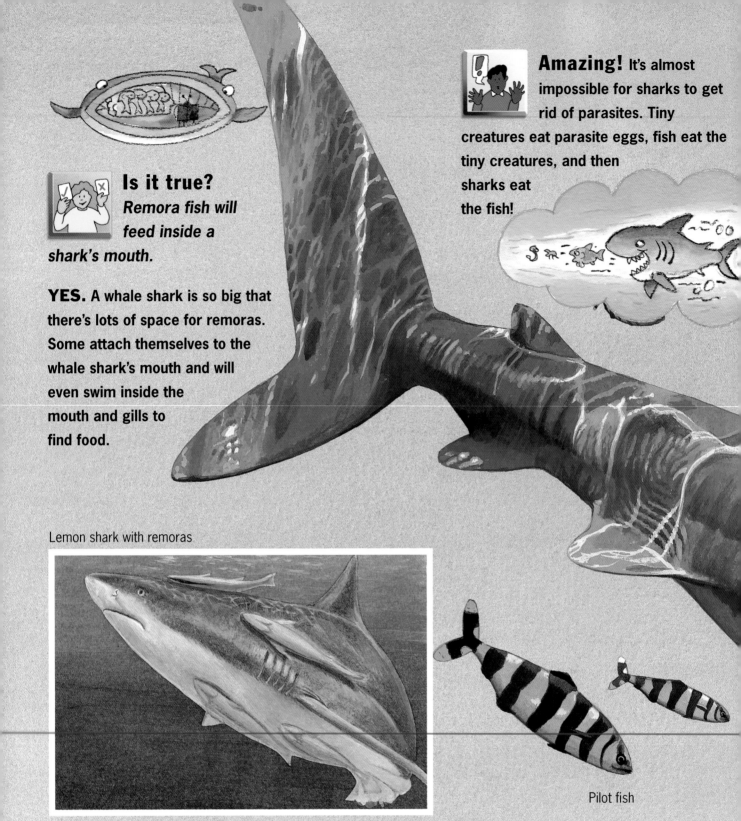

Amazing! It's almost impossible for sharks to get rid of parasites. Tiny creatures eat parasite eggs, fish eat the tiny creatures, and then sharks eat the fish!

Is it true?
Remora fish will feed inside a shark's mouth.

YES. A whale shark is so big that there's lots of space for remoras. Some attach themselves to the whale shark's mouth and will even swim inside the mouth and gills to find food.

Lemon shark with remoras

Pilot fish

What uses a sucker to hitch a ride?
Remoras are strange fish with large suction pads on the top of their heads. They use these to cling on to sharks. When they peel off to steal scraps, they must take care that the shark doesn't eat them.

Which travelers harm sharks?

Tiny creatures called parasites feed on a shark's skin, inside its guts and in its blood. Some even settle and feed on the surface of its eye, making it difficult for the shark to see.

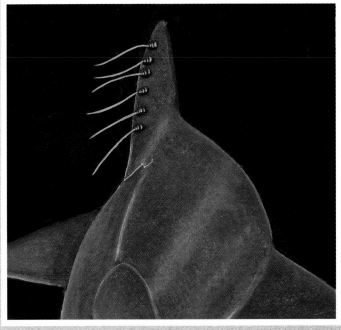

Parasites feeding on a shark's fin

What hides in a shark's shadow?

Just like remoras, pilot fish also travel with sharks. They're quick and agile as they swim alongside the shark. They hide in the shark's shadow, safe from their enemies, and dart out to snap up any left-overs from the latest kill.

? What can attack with its tail?

The thresher shark has a long and powerful tail, often longer than its main body, which it uses like a whip. Like dolphins, thresher sharks hunt in packs. They use their tails to stun fish or to round them up ready for attack.

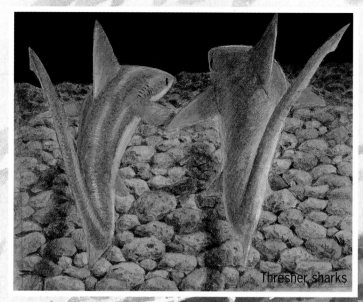
Thresher sharks

Seal

Mako shark

? Which is the fastest shark of all?

The mako shark can move through water as quickly as 45 mph. If an angler catches one, it sometimes leaps out of the water into the air as it tries to escape.

What can swallow a seal whole?

The great white shark, also known as 'white death', is a powerful predator that often swallows its prey whole. Luckily, it thinks that seals and sea lions are much tastier than human beings!

Amazing! Bull sharks are unusual because they prefer shark meat to other flesh. They're one of few sharks to spend time in fresh water. They swim up rivers and can enter lakes.

Great white shark

Is it true?
Sharks have to eat every day.

NO. After a good kill, a great white shark could last three months without food before it needs to eat again.

Which is the biggest fish in the world?

The biggest fish is also one of the most harmless, the whale shark. It measures 50 feet long and weighs about 13 tons. It swims slowly through the sea with its mouth open wide, filtering millions of tiny creatures from the water.

 Is it true?
You could hitch a ride on a whale shark.

YES. These gentle giants have been known to allow scuba divers to hang on to their fins and ride with them.

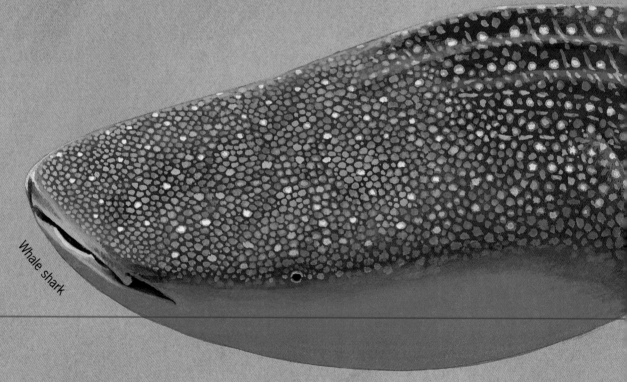

Whale shark

Amazing! Little is known about the megamouth. But we do know that it has luminous organs that give off a glow around its lips. Scientists think this may be to tempt tiny creatures into its mouth.

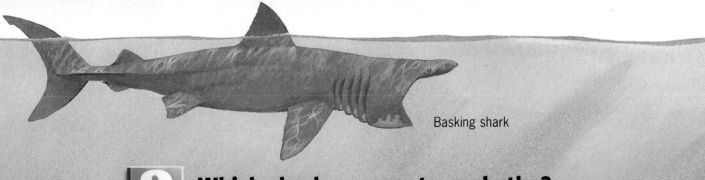

Basking shark

? Which shark appears to sunbathe?

Basking sharks spend much of their time wallowing at the ocean's surface, especially when it's sunny – probably because there's more food there on sunny days, not because they want a suntan!

Megamouth

? What has a huge mouth?

The megamouth shark lives in deep, dark seas. Like the whale shark, it swims with its enormous mouth wide open, filtering water for food. It is very rare and only a few have ever been seen.

Which shark has wings?

Angel sharks have very large pectoral fins, like an angel's wings. They spend much of their lives on the ocean floor, waiting for fish or shellfish to come along so they can snap them up.

Is it true?
Angel sharks look like monks.

YES. Angel sharks are also called monkfish because their heads are the same shape as a monk's hood.

Angel shark

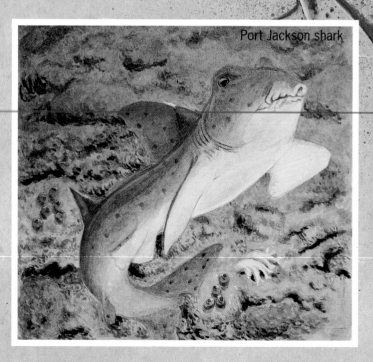

Port Jackson shark

What is a 'pig fish'?

The Port Jackson shark is known as the 'pig fish', or 'bulldog shark'. It has a blunt head and a squashed nose with very large nostrils for finding sea urchins and shellfish.

Which shark uses a disguise?

The wobbegong shark is a master of disguise. The coloring and markings of its flattened body help it blend into its surroundings on the seabed. It also has a 'beard' of skin around its mouth which looks just like seaweed to unsuspecting prey.

Amazing!

If a swell shark is attacked by a predator, it gulps down as much sea water as it can, and swells up like a balloon. It then jams itself into a crack in a rock where its enemy can't reach it.

Wobbegong

Which mysterious shark has a very long snout?

Goblin sharks were discovered 100 years ago and yet we still know very little about them. They live in deep water, and use their long, sensitive snouts to seek out prey.

Goblin shark

What has a head like a hammer?

The head of a hammerhead shark is spread out to form a T-shape with its body. Its eyes are on each end of the 'hammer'. As it swims, it swings its head from side to side so it can look around.

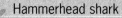

Hammerhead shark

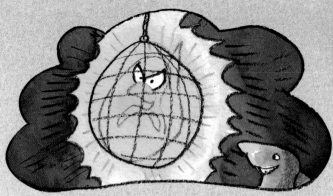

Is it true?
Cookiecutter sharks can glow.

YES. These small sharks have light organs on their undersides, which glow, maybe to persuade their prey to come close to them.

Seal wounded by cookiecutter

What bites chunks out of its prey?

Cookiecutter sharks are often happy with just a bite or two from their prey, which includes whales, seals and dolphins. The wounds they make with their small teeth are oval-shaped, a bit like a cookie.

Cookiecutter

Amazing!
Hammerhead sharks have few enemies and they feed alone. Yet they sometimes gather together in large 'schools', where hundreds all swim together.

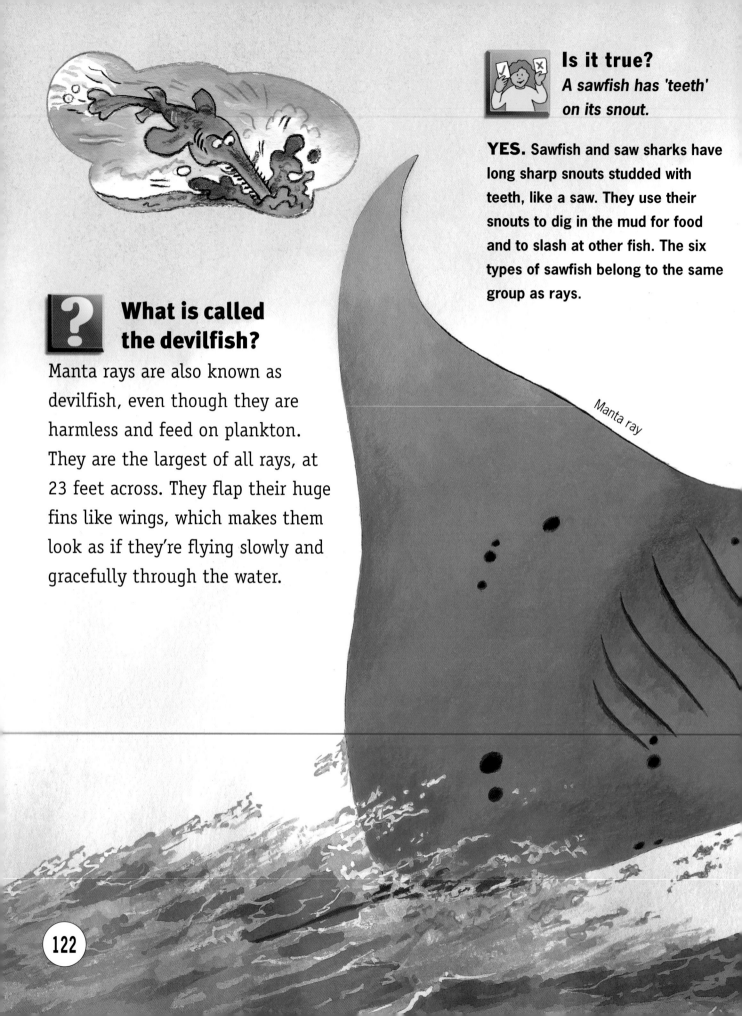

Is it true?
A sawfish has 'teeth' on its snout.

YES. Sawfish and saw sharks have long sharp snouts studded with teeth, like a saw. They use their snouts to dig in the mud for food and to slash at other fish. The six types of sawfish belong to the same group as rays.

Manta ray

What is called the devilfish?

Manta rays are also known as devilfish, even though they are harmless and feed on plankton. They are the largest of all rays, at 23 feet across. They flap their huge fins like wings, which makes them look as if they're flying slowly and gracefully through the water.

122

Electric ray

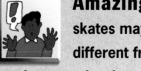

Which fish can shock?

The electric ray has special electric organs just behind its head. It gives off bursts of electricity to defend itself or to stun the fish it feeds on.

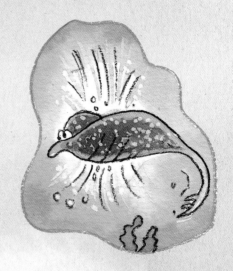

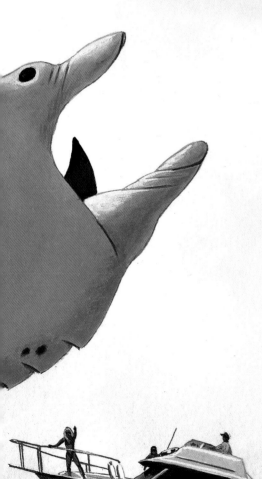

What has a sting on its tail?

Stingrays have poisonous spines on their whip-like tails. Some have one poisonous spine, others have several. They lie on the seabed with only their eyes and tail showing.

Stingray

Which eel becomes a fierce hunter?

When moray eels are young, they eat shrimps and tiny fish. But as they grow up, they learn to prey on larger and larger creatures.

Moray eel

Which tiny fish can strip an animal bare in minutes?

Piranhas live in rivers in South America where they hunt together in shoals of hundreds. With powerful jaws full of razor-sharp teeth, they may attack any large animal that enters the water.

Stonefish

❓ When is a stone not a stone?

When it's a stonefish. Stonefish are camouflaged so that it's almost impossible to see them amongst the rocks on the seabed. But sharp poisonous spines on their backs make them very dangerous to step on.

Piranha fish

Amazing! Many fish living in the cold, dark depths of the ocean look like monsters. They may have huge mouths full of sharp teeth, most are black and many can produce their own light.

125

Shark-proof bag

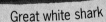

Amazing! In Australia in the 1930s, hundreds of sharks were caught in nets in just a few months. The numbers of many large sharks have gone down sharply all over the world because of hunting.

How can we prevent shark attacks?

Sharks have often attacked people who have survived shipwrecks or plane crashes far out at sea. Inflatable bags have been tested, which sharks tend to avoid. They can't detect moving limbs, electrical signals or blood inside them. Beaches can be protected by nets.

Great white shark

Is it true?
Nothing attacks a shark.

NO. Sharks will attack each other. They are also attacked by whales, and even dolphins who will group together to protect their young. But the biggest threat of all comes from people.

Why do sharks attack?

When a shark attacks, it is often because it mistakes a swimmer or surfer for a seal or other prey. About 100 shark attacks are recorded on people each year. Many of the victims survive.

Surfer on board

Seal

Shark cage

Who swims inside a cage?

Scientists studying dangerous sharks, such as the ocean white-tip and bull shark, often protect themselves inside a cage. The shark can bang the cage as much as it likes, but the diver is safe inside.

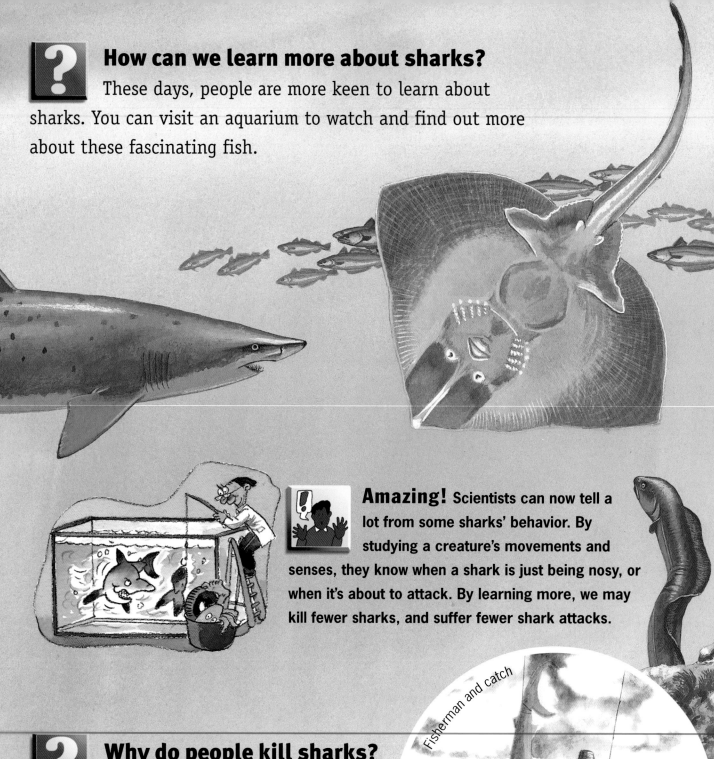

How can we learn more about sharks?

These days, people are more keen to learn about sharks. You can visit an aquarium to watch and find out more about these fascinating fish.

Amazing! Scientists can now tell a lot from some sharks' behavior. By studying a creature's movements and senses, they know when a shark is just being nosy, or when it's about to attack. By learning more, we may kill fewer sharks, and suffer fewer shark attacks.

Fisherman and catch

Why do people kill sharks?

People kill millions of sharks every year, some to protect swimmers, others for food or just for sport. If too many are killed, sharks might disappear altogether.

Which scientists dress like knights of old?

Scientists studying sharks sometimes wear chain-mail suits for protection. They may tag a shark's fins to learn how quickly and far it can travel.

Diver in chain-mail with blue shark

Is it true?
We've discovered all the sharks that exist.

NO. Megamouth was first seen in 1976. Scientists think that there might be more sharks waiting to be discovered in the depths of the oceans.

CHAPTER FIVE

BIRDS OF PREY

AND OTHER FEATHERED FRIENDS

? Which are the biggest birds?

The African ostrich can grow to over eight feet tall, which is much taller than the average man. The huge wandering albatross has the largest wingspan in the world, at nearly ten feet. Its long, pointed wings make it an excellent glider.

Ostrich

Amazing! There are around 9,000 different kinds of birds, in many colors, shapes and sizes. They live all over world, in steamy jungles, icy regions, by the sea, in towns, and some move from one area to another when they migrate.

Which are the smallest birds?

Hummingbirds are the smallest birds in world. The bee hummingbird of Cuba is no bigger than a bumblebee! Hummingbirds can flap their wings at up to 90 beats per second. They get their name from the humming sound their wings make.

Rufous hummingbird

Albatross

What are birds?

Birds all have two legs, two wings, a beak, they lay eggs and they are the only animals that have feathers. But not all birds can fly, and not all flying animals are birds.

Black-faced ant thrush

Is it true?
The first bird dates back to dinosaur times.

YES. Archaeopteryx is the earliest bird-like creature that we know of. It lived 150 million years ago. It had a head like a reptile, sharp teeth, a long tail and feathered wings.

133

Sparrowhawk

? What is a bird of prey?

Birds of prey catch and eat other animals. They are excellent hunters, with strong hooked beaks and sharp claws called talons, which they use to kill and tear at prey.

? Why are birds of prey good hunters?

The eyes of a bird of prey are different from other birds' eyes. They're very big, and face forwards so they can judge detail and distance well. A buzzard's eyes are as big as yours!

Buzzard

Amazing! Eagles can catch animals much bigger and heavier than themselves. The harpy eagle, which lives in South American jungles, is the biggest eagle of all. It has huge feet which it uses for grabbing and crushing monkeys and other animals.

Is it true?
Some birds eat eggs.

YES. The Egyptian vulture uses stones to break into its favorite food, ostrich eggs. Birds can have very fussy tastes. Bat hawks, for example, only eat bats. Some eagles eat fish, while others prefer snakes.

Osprey

How do ospreys hunt?

Ospreys fly high above the water looking for fish. When they spot one, they dive and enter the water feet-first to catch it. Their toes have tiny sharp spikes for gripping slippery fish.

? Which bird is a national symbol?

Eagles are the most powerful birds of prey and are often pictured on flags. The bald eagle is the national emblem of the USA, standing for strength and power.

Is it true?

The peregrine falcon can travel faster than an express train.

YES. When it spots a flying bird, the peregrine falcon folds its wings close to its body and dives at up to 220 mph.

Vultures

? Which birds are garbage collectors?

Vultures wait for creatures to die before rushing down to eat everything except the bones. They are very useful birds, getting rid of dead animals before they rot and spread disease.

Which birds can be trained?

Hawks and falcons can be trained by people.
Hawks fly fast and low over the ground when they hunt.
A long time ago the goshawk used to be trained to catch
food for people. It was known as the cook's bird.

Amazing! The Andean condor from
South America is the biggest bird of prey.
It has a wingspan of over nine feet and it
weighs up to 24 pounds.

Peregrine falcon
on falconer's glove

❓ Which owl is as white as snow?

The snowy owl lives in the icy Arctic. The male's feathers are pure white so that it can't be seen against the snow when it hunts for hares and lemmings. It has feathers on its feet to help keep its toes warm.

Snowy owl

❓ Why do owls hoot?

Owls make sounds to communicate with each other in the dark. Different owls have different calls. They also use a wide range of sounds, from clicks to grunts to hisses. When courting, some owls actually sing to each other!

138

How many types of owl are there?

Barn owl

There are 133 different kinds of owl, most of which hunt at night. Their special soft feathers mean they fly silently through the dark. With huge eyes and excellent hearing, they can swoop down to take prey by surprise.

Amazing! When an owl eats its prey there are usually parts it cannot digest, such as claws, teeth, beaks and fur. These parts are made into balls called pellets and passed back out through the bird's mouth.

Is it true?
An eagle owl's ears are on top of its head.

NO. The tufts on top of its head may look like ears, but they are only long feathers. The owl's real ears are under the feathers at the sides of its head.

Eagle owl

? Why do birds have feathers?

Birds have three different kinds of feathers: down to keep warm; body feathers to cover and protect; and flight feathers. Baby birds have down feathers and can't fly until they've grown all their flight feathers.

Albatross chick

Is it true?
All flamingos are pink.

NO. In the wild, flamingos are generally pink. Color from the food is absorbed and passes to the feathers. But in captivity, their feathers can turn white if they have a change of diet.

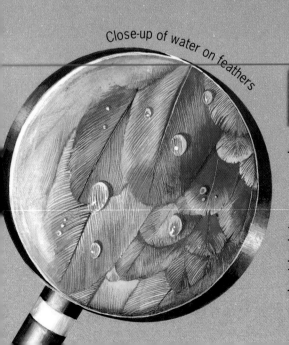
Close-up of water on feathers

? How do birds keep clean?

All birds comb, or preen, their feathers with their beaks and claws. Love birds preen each other. Most birds also spread oil on their feathers from a gland above the tail, which keeps them waterproof.

? Why are some feathers bright and others dull?

Many woodland birds, such as the tawny frogmouth, have dull feathers so that they can blend in with their background and keep safe. Male birds are often more brightly colored to attract a mate.

Tawny frogmouth and chick

Amazing!

Most birds have over 1,000 feathers and some birds have an enormous number. Swans have about 25,000 feathers – more than almost any other bird!

How do birds fly?

Birds need to be light but strong to fly. They flap their wings to take off and fly higher in air. As the wing flaps down, the flight feathers close against the air, which pushes the bird up and forward.

Reed warbler

What has to run to take off?

Swans are too big and heavy to leap into the air. Instead they have to run along the surface of the water, flapping their powerful wings to get enough speed to take off.

Swan

Amazing!

Big seabirds glide on air currents, sometimes not landing for weeks. Other birds can stay in the air for months, while swifts can spend years in the air, only landing to nest and mate.

Kestrel

? What can fly and yet stay in the same spot?

Kestrels are experts at hovering. They fly into the wind and beat their wings very quickly. This lets them stay in the same position as they search for prey below.

Is it true?

Birds can only fly forwards.

NO. Hummingbirds are special. They can fly forwards, sideways, backwards and hover on the spot by flapping their wings very quickly!

? Whose beak can hold more than its stomach?

A pelican has a beak with a stretchy pouch which can hold far more fish than its stomach! It scoops fish from the water using its beak like a fishing net.

! Amazing!

A woodpecker uses its unusual beak to drill for insects, to make holes in dying trees to use as nests, and to hammer on a tree to mark its territory.

144

Why do birds have beaks?

Birds use their beaks to catch and hold food, to make nests and to preen themselves. They have different beaks because they eat different food. The toucan uses its enormous beak to pull fruits from delicate branches.

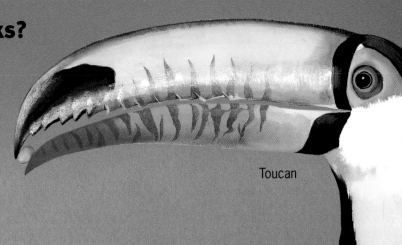

Toucan

Is it true?

Birds have teeth.

NO. Birds cannot chew, so they grind food up with a gizzard inside their bodies, and sometimes by swallowing small stones too.

Yellow-headed parrot

What climbs with its beak?

Parrots usually live in big noisy groups in tropical forests. They have short, curved powerful beaks for cracking nuts and seeds. Some parrots have beaks so strong that they can even use them to pull themselves up trees.

145

Why do ducks have webbed feet?

Water birds have skin between their toes. Their feet are like paddles, helping them move easily through the water. They can also walk on mud without sinking in.

African jacana

Amazing! Jacanas are water birds that live in tropical places. Their very long toes allow them to step on water plants without sinking. They are sometimes called 'lily-trotters'.

Redhead duck

Is it true?
Birds stand on one leg when they've hurt their foot.

NO. When a bird stands on one leg, it is keeping the other foot warm, tucked up under its feathers.

Heron

❓ What has legs like stilts?

Herons and storks have very long legs which look like stilts. They are ideal for standing or wading in shallow water, where the birds use their long beaks to catch fish and frogs.

Budgerigar

❓ Why don't birds fall when they sleep?

Birds have a long tendon attached to each toe. When they rest on branches or another perch, they bend their legs and their toes lock around the perch.

? What hangs upside down to court?

When the male bird of paradise wants to attract a female it hangs upside down to show off its beautiful tail. Females and chicks are often dull compared to males so that they can remain safely hidden in the trees.

Male blue bird of paradise

Amazing! Great crested grebes dance on the water in front of each other for several weeks before they finally mate and pair for life. They can perform four separate complicated dance routines.

What hypnotizes with its 'eyes'?

The male peacock has a fan made of beautiful jeweled feathers. The 'eyes' on the feathers fascinate its mate, the peahen. By looking at them, she can tell that he is a healthy male to choose.

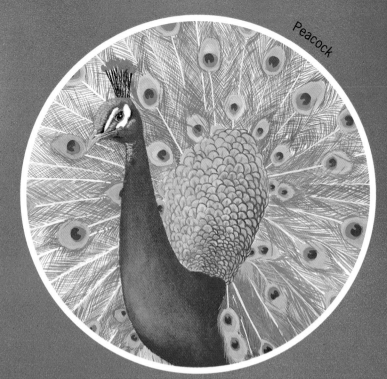
Peacock

Is it true?

Birds stay with a mate for only one season.

NO. Some birds, including swans, gannets and golden eagles, find a mate and stay with that same bird for the rest of their lives.

What attracts its mate with a red balloon?

The male frigate bird has a bright red pouch under his chin. When he wants to find a mate, he puffs it out like a balloon. If the female is impressed, she rubs her head against the pouch.

Frigate birds

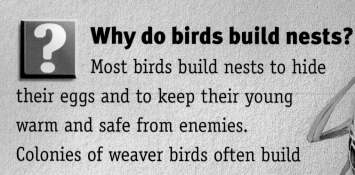

? Why do birds build nests?

Most birds build nests to hide their eggs and to keep their young warm and safe from enemies. Colonies of weaver birds often build several nests in the same tree.

Black-headed weaver birds

Hummingbird's nest

 Amazing! Some nests are huge. An eagle's nest or eyrie is so big that you could lie down in it! Some birds, such as the hummingbird, make tiny nests. The bee hummingbird's nest is the same size as a thimble.

Thrushes

? Why do birds sit on their eggs?

Birds sit on their eggs to keep them warm while the baby birds inside grow. If the eggs get cold, the babies inside will die, so birds don't leave their eggs alone for long.

Is it true?

Nests are birds' homes where they sleep at night.

NO. Birds only use nests for laying eggs and raising their chicks. They rest at night in hedges, trees or holes.

Do birds' eggs all look the same?

Birds' eggs are often colored or patterned for camouflage. The guillemot's eggs are also an unusual shape. They are pointed at one end so that if nudged, they spin in a circle instead of rolling off a cliff.

What do newly hatched birds look like?

The young of tree-nesting birds are naked and blind at first. Their parents have to look after them, and they are always hungry! They open their beaks wide and call loudly, which forces the parents to feed them.

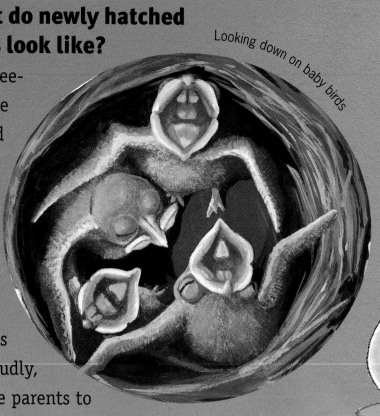

Looking down on baby birds

Amazing! The hummingbird lays the world's smallest eggs. Each is only the size of your fingernail. Compared to this, an ostrich egg is huge, and thousands of times heavier.

Grebe with young

What sits on its mother's back?

Baby grebes can swim soon after they hatch. When they get cold or tired, they sit on their mother's back to warm up and have a rest.

? Which father sits on his eggs until they hatch?

The male ostrich makes eggs with up to twelve different females. The females all lay their eggs in same nest. The male then sits on them himself until they hatch. Many types of male bird, including pigeons, take it in turns with the female to sit on the eggs.

Ostriches and chicks

Is it true?
A duckling could mistake you for its mother.

YES. A duckling thinks that the first creature it sees after hatching is its mother. If you were around, that would be you!

Which bird calls to find its nest?

When a male gannet has caught fish for his mate and young, he must call out and wait for the female's reply before he can find them amongst all the other gannets.

Gannets

Why do birds sing?

Birds sing most of all during the breeding season. A male bird sings to attract a mate, or to tell other birds to keep away from his territory. Males and females also call to warn other birds that an enemy is near, such as a cat or a human.

Magpie lark

? Which birds copy sounds?

Some birds are natural mimics. This means they can copy sounds, such as the telephone ringing or even human speech. The mynah bird used to be popular as a caged pet because of this talent. Australian lyrebirds can even imitate a chainsaw!

Amazing! The African grey parrot is a real chatterbox. It can learn up to 800 different words, but it doesn't know what they mean!

Superb lyrebird

Is it true?

Birds can sing very high notes.

YES. Many birds can sing notes too high for us to hear! There is a wide range of beautiful birdsong, full of high and low notes.

Pigeon

? Which bird finds its way home?

Pigeons have a great sense of direction. Scientists think they use the position of the Sun, Moon and stars, the Earth's magnetic pull and landmarks. People race pigeons as a hobby, because they usually find their way home safely.

Snow geese

Amazing! The Arctic tern travels right across the Earth, from the Arctic to Antarctica and back again each year. That's a round trip of 22,000 miles. It keeps up its energy by eating fish as it flies.

Is it true?

Migrating birds must eat as they travel.

NO. Many kinds of birds do not eat during their migration. Instead they eat large amounts of food before they leave in order to survive the trip.

? Which birds fly in a 'V' pattern?

Geese migrate in groups like this, or they fly together in long chains. The younger birds learn which way to go by following the older birds in front.

? Do migrating birds remember the way?

Some migrating birds use familiar landmarks such as islands or mountains to find their way. Swifts often fly from the other side of the world back to the same nest each year.

Swift

What was a dodo?

Have you heard the expression 'as dead as a dodo'? Dodos were strange-looking, heavy birds that could not fly. They lived on islands in the Indian Ocean until sailors hunted the very last one. Sadly, they have been extinct since 1800.

Dodo

Kiwi

What has invisible wings?

Kiwis are flightless birds whose wings are so tiny that you cannot see them. They have long whiskers, no tail and a good sense of smell. They hunt at night for worms and insects.

Which bird 'flies' underwater?

Penguins are water birds which cannot fly. They live in the chilly Antarctic. They slide on snow and ice using their bellies as toboggans. But in water they are very graceful, using their wings as flippers as they swim along catching fish.

King penguins

Is it true?
Penguins argue with their wings.

YES. Penguins live close together. When they squabble with each other, they flap their wings and jab their beaks to help make their point!

Amazing! Ostriches cannot fly, but they can run very quickly indeed. The African ostrich can sprint along at 40 mph! They live in dry grasslands and may have to travel a long way for food.

CHAPTER SIX

WILD CATS

AND OTHER DANGEROUS PREDATORS

Grizzly bear

What do cats, dogs and bears have in common?

They are all mammals. This means that they are covered with cosy fur and feed their young with mother's milk. Cats, dogs and bears are also all carnivores, which means they eat meat. To do this, they have special sharp, pointy teeth, called canines.

Is it true?

Cats, dogs and bears are the only carnivores in the world.

NO. Many other mammals, such as hyenas, weasels, raccoons and humans eat meat. So do other animals – birds of prey, some reptiles and sharks in the sea.

Great white shark